To Sharon ~
Blessings on you!

Peg Carlson

This is a book for seekers...

...seeking
to life

Those seeking
deeper relationship with God

Those seeking
a better attitude toward themselves.

Glorify God & Enjoy Him Forever

Peg Rankin

Regal Books

A Division of GL Publications
Ventura, California, U.S.A.

Other good reading:
Yet Will I Trust Him by Peg Rankin
If Being a Christian Is So Great, Why Do I Have the Blahs?
    by John A. Dobbert
Reaching Your Possibilities Through Commitment by
    Gerald W. Marshall

The foreign language publishing of all Regal books is under the direction of GLINT. GLINT provides financial and technical help for the adaptation, translation and publishing of books in more than 85 languages for millions of people worldwide.

For more information write: GLINT, P.O. Box 6688, Ventura, California 93006.

Published by Regal Books
A Division of GL Publications
Ventura, California 93006
Printed in U.S.A.

Library of Congress Catalog Card No. 81-51742
ISBN 0-8307-0796-4

Contents

Dedication

This book is lovingly dedicated to John Palmer, who precipitated my quest for God's glory.

With a special thanks to Lee for his typing of the manuscript, to Dr. Kraft for her medical consultation, and to Judy for her critical analysis of the first draft . . . and the second draft . . . and the third draft . . .

Preface

Reader, I have a few questions for you to chew on. Did you ever stop to wonder what you are doing here on this earth? What would you consider to be the purpose for your existence? When you think about what you do each day, what would you give as the motive for your actions?

We don't have to ask too many questions of this nature before we realize how challenging they are, do we? Such queries really provoke our thinking. In fact, they stimulate us to bore through the superficialities of our lives very quickly and get right to the core of the matter.

When I personally have the opportunity to probe people's minds in this area, the answers I receive to these questions usually reveal three levels of thinking: (1) "I'm living for myself"; (2) "I'm living for others"; or (3) "I'm living for God."

How would you verbalize answers to the above series of questions? Would you say something like this: "I'm out for number one and make no bones about it. I have a good job, nice clothes, a comfortable home, and a late model car. And I intend to keep what I have. To stay in shape I maintain a regular exercise program. I jog three times a week, golf on Saturdays, and play tennis on Sundays. I take a couple of evening courses on self-improvement. I want to get all out of life that I can." Would you answer like that?

Well, if you would, you fit into the mold of a great portion of the western world. Your answer is not necessarily a bad one; self-fulfillment and self-improvement are worthy pursuits. But they should never be allowed to become your primary motive for living. The reason is that they are not the purpose for which the God of all creation designed you.

Perhaps you would answer more nobly: "My life is dedicated to others—family, friends, church. I'm working 12, 14 hours a day just to put food on the table. Two nights a week I sponsor clubs for kids. And on Sundays I teach Sunday School and sing in the choir. I give and give and give until there's no more in me to come out."

That's quite a purpose for living—very commendable, I think. But it is still not the reason why God made you. In fact, of the three motives people give for their actions (self, others, and God), only the last one is valid eternally.

God made us for Himself and for Himself alone. His purpose for our existence is that we might manifest His glory—so the Bible states and so most Christian confessions of faith reiterate. Therefore our daily prayer should be, "Lord, today it is my desire to be a true reflection of you."

Unfortunately, most people, even those of us who call ourselves Christians, spend too much time on the first level of existence: living for self. There are some, of course, who manage to graduate to the second level: living for others. But there are disturbingly few people on the third level: living primarily for the glory of God. I wonder why. Is it that we do not know our reason for having been created? Or if we do know it, is it perhaps that we don't know how to put our principles into practice?

The following pages have been written for two purposes: (1) to reemphasize our purpose for living and (2) to suggest some tangible ways for fulfilling it. After all, if our chief end and purpose is to glorify God, then how in the nitty-gritty world of everyday routine are we supposed to attain such a lofty goal? This is the *real* question.

Before you read the book it might be helpful to stop for a moment to take an honest inventory of your own spiritual desires. Are you sick of mere, routine existence? Are you searching for a motive that will revolutionize your actions? Do you want your life to really count for God?

If so, read on. Over and over again you will be admonished to glorify God and enjoy Him forever. Along with these admonitions will be practical suggestions to help your desires become reality. The suggestions will fall into four categories: (1) We will see the necessity of developing a right orientation toward God; (2) then it follows that we will need to cultivate a proper attitude toward ourselves; (3) next we will examine some of the dangers that would divert us from our goal; and (4) we will learn how to touch other lives with the same holy purpose that we ourselves have embraced.

By the time you finish reading this book I hope you will be as excited as I am about facing every new day. I also hope that your enthusiasm will rub off in very practical ways in your home, in your place of business, in your church, and in your community. If God could turn the world upside down through a handful of early disciples who were sold out to the purpose of bringing Him glory, what do you think He might choose to accomplish through Christians today if we all really got hold of the same life-changing principle?

PART I

A Right Orientation Toward God

ONE
Beholding Him

TWO
Receiving Him

THREE
Yielding to Him

FOUR
Communing with Him

FIVE
Becoming His Channel

ONE
Beholding Him

"I really want to glorify God with my life, but I don't know where to start. Is there anything you can suggest to point me in the right direction? Make it simple, please. I feel like a baby who is on the verge of learning how to walk."

What a precious question to ask—so sincere, so honest, and so straightforward. And how wonderful to have an answer right from the Lord Himself! Pull that Bible down off the shelf, separate its pages, and begin to read about God. This is your answer in all of its simplicity. Maybe it is so simple that up until now it has escaped you. But it is not so simple that it cannot change your life.

Reading the Bible is the first step in becoming rightly oriented toward life because it gives you a proper orientation toward the Author of your life—God Himself. Once you catch a glimpse of Him in all His awesome glory, you can never be the same again. You will find yourself exalting Him, honoring Him, worshiping Him, praising Him, and reflecting Him—which is precisely what "glorifying God" actually entails. Such a response should occur quite naturally in your life if you only start in the right place: in the life-changing Word of God.

As you read the Scriptures, you will see the various ways that God has revealed Himself to man. In each of these divine manifestations you will probably notice a recurring phenomenon: God often underscores His presence visibly. I believe He wants to underscore it just as visibly in the lives of Christians today. The Bible calls these visible manifestations of God His "glory."

Let us examine some Old Testament examples of this glory. When the Lord was alone in the heavens, long before He created the earth and its inhabitants, even before He made the angels, He manifested His presence in a light too marvelous for description. To be sure, there were no beings present to behold this glory; but their absence did not take away from the fact that it was there. God is light and light must shine whether there is anybody present to witness it or not. So the glory of God lit His habitation with warmth and beauty long before anything else ever existed.

Then the Lord flung the stars into space, billions upon billions of them—all quiet reflections of His glory. They were wonderfully radiant indeed but quite unappreciated in their majesty until God formed eyes to behold them. The first beings privileged to witness the beauty of the heavens were the angels, whom God created to be messengers of His glory. Those who were obedient to their purpose are still singing His praises today: "Glory, glory, glory, Lord God of hosts." Their songs will resound throughout eternity.

In due time the Lord created the earth and inhabitants to walk upon it. They too saw the glory of God's perfect creation, and to them also was given the awesome responsibility of reflecting it. But for reasons known only to themselves, these earth inhabitants deliberately rebelled against yielding themselves to the purpose of their great Creator. Instead, they chose to make themselves like little gods, controlling their own destinies in life, ignoring God's glory altogether.

God's glory, however, is something which cannot be

dimmed. The Lord selected a special people, the Israelites, to whom to manifest it in some very special ways. As they were wandering through the wilderness on their way to the Promised Land, God said to them, "In the morning . . . ye shall see the glory of the Lord" (Exod. 16:7). And He was very faithful to that promise. For many mornings, and evenings too, the Israelites saw God's presence in a visible, physical way. It went before them as a cloud in the day and as a pillar of fire at night.

Another physical manifestation of God's glory occurred on top of Mount Sinai. When Moses received the Ten Commandments God's radiance so surrounded the transaction that when Moses came down off the mount, the people covered his face with a "vail." The Bible says that "the children of Israel could not look steadily at the face of Moses because of the glory of his countenance" (2 Cor. 3:7). Reader, how would you react if somebody came up to you and said, "The glory of God is so visible in your face I have to avert my eyes for fear of being blinded"? Wouldn't you be thrilled through and through that God could actually be seen in you? I would. But we must remember how the radiance in Moses' face got there: through a confrontation with the God of glory Himself.

The glory of God showed itself to the Israelites in at least one other way. When they built their Tabernacle of worship according to God's detailed instructions, they constructed a special room called the holy of holies. It was here that the ark of the covenant was placed, containing the law which Moses had received directly from God on Mount Sinai. The ark was covered by cherubim of gold. And between the cherubim God's glory came to rest—visible, physical, and quite obvious to any who were privileged by God to see it. The psalmist says, "O Shepherd of Israel, . . . thou that dwellest between the cherubims, shine forth" (Ps. 80:1). To that prayer I would like to add my own request: "Lord, shine forth again today. And let it be through the likes of me."

In all of these Old Testament situations God visibly manifested His glory. Most of the men who saw it, however, kept missing the point that they were supposed to reflect it. They continued to pursue their own goals in life, shaking their fist at God's purpose for their existence. And for several silent years God did not show Himself at all, leaving men to wander in darkness.

It was into this state of desperation that Jesus the Saviour stepped, "And we beheld His glory, the glory as of the only begotten of the Father, full of grace and truth" (John 1:14). Everything about His life radiated the presence of God. The angels heralded His birth, singing, "Glory to God in the highest" (Luke 2:14). The Father witnessed His baptism, proclaiming Him a Son in whom He was "well-pleased" (Matt. 3:17). Christ Himself tailored His every action according to His earthly purpose. He spoke to the glory of God, He performed miracles to the glory of God, and He died to the glory of God. In fact, right before His earthly life was over, He said to the Father, "I have glorified You on the earth. I have finished the work which You have given Me to do. And now, O Father, glorify Me together with Yourself, with the glory which I had with You before the world was" (John 17:4,5). God did. When Christ rose from the dead His disciples "saw His glory" (Luke 9:32). And when He returns to earth to consummate His redemptive plan we shall see Him "coming in the clouds with great power and glory" (Mark 13:26).

A victory celebration will be held in heaven. Angels will surround God's throne, "ten thousand times ten thousand" of them, singing the praises of Christ: "Worthy is the Lamb who was slain to receive power and riches and wisdom, and strength and honor and glory and blessing"

(Rev. 5:11,12). Joining the scene will be "a great multitude which no one could number, of all nations, tribes, peoples, and tongues." They will be "clothed with white robes, with palm branches in their hands" (Rev. 7:9), and will stand before the Lamb, singing their praises of His marvelous acts.

This scene is a thrilling consummation of history, an explosive burst of God's glory, but we don't have to wait to experience it. We can taste a little now. For this great God of glory is still making His presence known and still expecting us to reflect His radiance.

The most common way that God reveals Himself to man is through His written Word. In the free world we have ready access to the Scriptures, even to many versions and paraphrases; but how often we neglect to pick them up and read them! Sometimes we even forget that they are there.

I once heard a speaker challenge his audience to open the Bible and start reading at the beginning, marking the phrase "the glory of God" with a yellow highlighter every time it occurred. My ears immediately perked up. So, praise God, did my will.

When the message was over I vowed to take the speaker up on his challenge. But best intentions get sidetracked sometimes and it took me 15 years to get down to the task of actually tracing the glory of God from one end of the Bible to the other. By the time I got around to it the speaker had been transported to his heavenly home and was actually experiencing in all its fullness the marvelous glory of God. And I, admittedly, was now more prepared to receive the treasure God had for me than I would have been if I had begun my task immediately after hearing the message. But 15 whole years! What a delay! Why in the world did I wait so long? I'm just thankful the Lord kept that vow in my heart all those years. For as I ran my highlighter over the last mention of "glory" in the book of Revelation I was so stuffed with blessing I could hardly contain myself.

I had found personal admonitions all through the Bible—at least I took them personally. When David said, "Give unto the Lord the glory due unto his name" (Ps. 29:2), I knew I wanted to do exactly that. When God promised, "I will deliver thee, and thou shalt glorify me" (Ps. 50:15), I felt that since I too had been "delivered" many times I wanted to obey the same admonition which God had given the psalmist. Then when the Lord mentioned "every one that is called by my name: for I have created him for my glory" (Isa. 43:7), I knew *I* was included in that purpose.

Even today as I leaf through my Bible the blessing of my spiritual exercise repeats itself all over again. I read, "You were bought at a price; therefore glorify God in your body and in your spirit, which are God's" (1 Cor. 6:20). And then, just in case I still have a question about my purpose for living, I come across the clincher: "Therefore, whether you eat or drink, or whatever you do, do all to the glory of God" (1 Cor. 10:31).

Phrases referring to the glory of God do not, however, occur on every page of God's Word. They do not even occur in every book. They are abundant in the Psalms, in the Prophets, in the Gospels, and in the Epistles; yet in the historical accounts, when God's people are rebelling against their holy calling, there are few, if any, highlighted words at all. In fact, whole passages become chronicles of cold, factual history—history of men who were blind to God's purpose for their lives.

I don't want my life to be that kind of waste. I don't want to be a mere statistic in man's legal and historical documents, mentioned as having been born, having existed, and having died—that's all. I want to behold the glory of God to such a degree that it becomes a visible reality in my life. Moreover, I want to transmit that glory to others so that the world might know that God is real. How about you? Do you share that same desire?

This question brings us back to the challenge of *actual-ly applying in our lives the truth we understand with our minds.* How in practice does one begin living his life for the glory of God? As I have already suggested, is it not by first beholding that glory in all of its awesome majesty? At least that's how the prophet Isaiah became dedicated to God's purpose for his life.

The Scriptures imply that one day, when Isaiah was in a state of great perplexity, he became burdened to draw away from his problems and meditate upon the Lord. So that is what he did. The Lord then revealed Himself to Isaiah with a direct confrontation of His glory. This is Isaiah's account of what happened:

"In the year that King Uzziah died I saw also the Lord sitting upon a throne, high and lifted up, and his train filled the temple. Above it stood the seraphims: each one had six wings; with twain he covered his face, and with twain he covered his feet, and with twain he did fly. And one cried unto another, and said, Holy, holy, holy, is the Lord of hosts: the whole earth is full of his glory" (Isa. 6:1-3).

Once Isaiah had this confrontation with God, he then had a confrontation with himself. Seeing how far short he had fallen of his holy purpose for living, he exclaimed: "Woe is me! for I am undone; because I am a man of unclean lips, and I dwell in the midst of a people of unclean lips: for mine eyes have seen the King, the Lord of hosts" (Isa. 6:5).

The next step was for Isaiah to receive God's purging which, in this case, came by means of an angel. The angel touched Isaiah's lips with a hot coal from off the altar so that from this point on those lips might proclaim a brand new message. Instead of doubt, despair, frustration, and blasphemy, there would be the abundant praise of God's glory. The angel said: "Lo, this hath touched thy lips; and thine iniquity is taken away, and thy sin purged" (Isa. 6:7).

After these confrontations both with God and with himself, Isaiah had a confrontation with the world. He immediately realized that he had an obligation to all the people within his sphere of influence that they might be challenged with the same holy purpose which he himself had just received, that they too might know what it means not only to see God's glory and to receive God's glory but to pass that glory on to others. Convicted, Isaiah yielded his life to this purpose. He had discovered and surrendered to his destiny.

I want to emphasize the fact that this great change in Isaiah's orientation toward life took place only because he first beheld the Lord in all His awesome majesty. So, if you want to experience a change in your own life, do what Isaiah did. Set aside a few moments out of your day to think about God and Him alone. To channel your thoughts properly, pick up a Bible and begin reading. Read Isaiah or the Psalms or the Gospels or the Epistles. But read something.

As you read, ask God to reveal Himself to you. He will. He loves a searching heart. But make sure you let God show Himself to you in His own way and in His own time. And as you view your Lord, expect to see yourself also. This last picture may not be as pleasing as the first, but it is certainly just as necessary; for it prepares you to take the next step in your spiritual pilgrimage: that of receiving the God of glory into your very own life.

Study Questions

1. Name some of the various ways that God reveals His glory.

2. What does it mean to "glorify God" with your life?

3. Can you think of any people whose lives were changed by beholding the Lord in His glory?

TWO
Receiving Him

As thrilling a practice as beholding the Lord may prove to be, you can't just sit and contemplate His glory for the rest of your life, not if you want any change to occur within you, that is. After beholding Him, you must receive Him. But what does "receiving the Lord" mean? Well, the event is described in many ways by many people. I would like to tell you how I personally received Christ and then explain to you how a similar experience can be yours.

I was reared in a "church-going" home. When I was about 13 years old I responded to an evangelist's invitation "to come down to the front of the church and receive Jesus Christ as your Saviour." Although I was sincere at the time, I did not realize that "receiving Christ" meant receiving God's purpose for my life. I thought I could continue to live as I pleased, adding a few Christian principles here and there wherever they conveniently fit into my life-style. Therefore, because my emphasis was still on myself instead of on the Lord, there was no real change in my behavior. I was a "professor" of Christ but not a "possessor." Nor was I possessed by Him.

When it came time to go to college I chose a secular school. While I was there I took several courses in religion. I sat under professors who did not believe that the Bible was the divinely inspired Word of God. They said, "Take what is pleasing to you, and leave out what you don't like." They presented the atonement of Jesus Christ on Calvary as having several viewpoints. They said, "Take whichever one you can best support intellectually."

Well, I got A's in those courses and graduated from that school with honors, but inside I was desperately confused. I had been given no absolutes, only a series of alternatives. And I didn't know which one was right.

I married and accompanied my husband to Virginia where he was serving for two years with the United States Army. At that time we were on a terribly hectic schedule with our day starting at 3:30 in the morning.

Usually I would get up with my husband (things have changed a bit since then) and clean the apartment, starch his uniforms, and then go teach a full day of school. I guess you can imagine that by the time the weekend rolled around we were totally exhausted. We would go to church on Sunday morning only when we could drag ourselves out of bed. More often than not, we didn't make it. We never attended a night service. We never went to Sunday School. And we wouldn't have been caught dead in a midweek service. Furthermore, we never touched our Bibles.

But, you know, I was bothered. I found myself wandering through the maze of existence without any direction. What was the significance of living supposed to be? I can remember lying awake at night, searching. My very soul cried out, "Oh, God, why was I born?"

Just about this time, my husband faced that all-important decision, his first job. He talked to one of his army buddies who suggested interviewing a certain New England-based company where his brother-in-law was employed.

So my husband did. When the job offers came, one was from this New England-based company. I looked at the offers from a woman's viewpoint and figured he'd just naturally take the job with the biggest salary. But, you know, he didn't. He took the job with the least salary of all. In fact, the salary was nonexistent. He was on straight commission.

My husband felt that this situation would offer the challenge he was looking for in a job; and so, with an expectant attitude, we moved to New England. After renting for a while we decided that it would be economically feasible for us to invest our small savings in a small home. Since my husband's sales territory was the North Shore of the Boston area, any place in the general vicinity would do. So, we got in the car one Sunday afternoon and just started to wander around the area.

We came upon the very lovely town of Lexington, Massachusetts, which endeared itself to us right away. Entering the first realtor's establishment we saw, we told the salesgirl inside what we wanted in a home. Then we told her what we could afford, and she just laughed. So we got back in the car and wandered around some more. Before long we came upon a darling split-level home that advertised itself as an "Open House." Unfortunately it was still in historic Lexington where the prices were sky high. But the house was so attractive that we decided to investigate.

Once inside, we met another realtor. Listening intently to our problem, he said, "I think I have an answer for you. I have a house like this one in the town of Burlington. That's where young people start out. The house is a little smaller, but it costs only two-thirds as much. Would you like to see it?"

We didn't need a second invitation. We almost flew into his car and drove over to Burlington, Massachusetts. Turning onto a street called Upland Road, we passed about seven houses or so and then we saw it—a darling little split-level nestled back among the trees. We fell in love with the Burlington house at first sight.

To make a long story short, we invested our small savings in that little house, set up housekeeping, and got to know our neighbors. Almost four months later, a very disturbing rumor started to circulate through the neighborhood: a minister was moving in at the end of the street. Everybody was speculating on what effect his presence would have on the life-style of our neighborhood.

Little did I realize what was ahead! One day while I was upstairs changing the baby's diaper, I noticed a man in a business suit approaching my house. I thought, *Oh, just another salesman. I won't bother to go to the door.*

But while I was looking out the window I must have poked the baby with a pin because he started to scream for all he was worth. I could no longer pretend I was not at home. I would *have* to go to the door. But I was annoyed. So before I went downstairs I put on my what-right-have-you-got-to-interrupt-my-day face. Then I opened the door.

The man outside was cordial to me even though I wasn't cordial to him. He introduced himself as John Palmer and handed me his business card. I looked at it and thought to myself, *Hmm . . . just what I thought. A salesman! But he's not selling anything salesmen usually sell. He's peddling religion.* At least that's how I looked at it then.

When I looked at his card again I noticed that the denomination he was representing was different from the one I'd been brought up in. So I immediately got suspicious. I thought he wanted to change my religion. And I thought he wanted my money. I didn't have any, but I thought he wanted it anyway.

When I looked at his card a third time, I noticed a very strange word: missionary. Having been accustomed to church language, I certainly thought I knew what a missionary is. A missionary is someone who goes to a foreign land to convert the heathen to Jesus Christ. Then what was this man doing on Upland Road in Burlington, Massachusetts, in the United States of America?

I soon found out. He told me he was starting a neighborhood Bible class and was canvassing the neighborhood to see who would be interested in attending. Well, you know, it's amazing how the mind works. I put way in the back of my mind the fact that I had spent sleepless nights wondering why I was born. And I brought to the front those A's I had gotten in those religion courses in college. I thought to myself, *I'll betcha I can give him a run for his money!* And that was the attitude with which I attended my first neighborhood Bible study.

I dragged my husband along with me to that first meeting. When we got there, there were about a dozen people present. After John Palmer introduced all of us to each other, we sat down. Then Reverend Palmer started the class in a way that really threw me. He called us "dearly beloved." Now I don't know how that phrase strikes you, but my own husband doesn't even call me "dearly beloved." I concluded that this teacher must be some kind of nut.

I watched him closely. Then I was convinced: he *was* some kind of nut. I watched him take three handkerchiefs out of his pocket—a red one and two white ones. And then he made a sandwich. He put the red one in between the two white ones, then he blew his nose! I had never seen anybody blow his nose on three handkerchiefs before—at once. But after I heard the explosion, I realized why he used three. To this day, however, I haven't figured out the significance of the red one in the middle. He had a few other interesting habits too, like wearing long johns that kept creeping below his pant legs. The farther down they got, the more fascinated I became.

Anyway, believe it or not, we finally got down to business that night. John Palmer told us that he considered the Bible to be God's divinely inspired Word. We would be studying the Gospel of John, a chapter a week. At the end of each chapter we would have an opportunity to ask questions.

This is what I was waiting for. So, while Reverend Palmer was going through the first chapter of the Gospel of John, my mind was going round and round. By the time he finished I had a whole list of questions. I picked out the most philosophical, the most difficult to answer, and threw it at him.

He answered it—and the question that followed—and the question that followed—not from what he *thought* the answer was, but from what the Word of God *said* the answer was. And he showed it to me to prove it.

As the days grew into weeks and the weeks into months, I began to admire John Palmer. He was totally dedicated, completely sincere. And he had a fantastic knowledge of the Word of God, at least in my eyes. I'm sure I was secretly wishing I had the command of the Bible he had. I never would have admitted it, but I'm sure I was coveting his knowledge. I really admired him.

I didn't like him any better, though, because by this time he was really bugging me. I began to realize that he had something I didn't have. Furthermore, I realized that he *knew* he had something I didn't have. The latter realization was driving me crazy.

One day Reverend Palmer came to my house, as he was in the habit of doing by now. He said, "Peg, you've been asking me a lot of questions over the last few weeks. Do you mind if I ask you a question?"

I said, "I don't mind."

He said, "Do you promise not to get mad?"

I thought, *Oh brother! I wonder what's coming now.*

But I told him, "OK, I promise I won't get mad."

He asked, "Are you saved?"

And I got mad! I said, "Well, I want you to know that I'm a baptized member of a church and I walked an aisle at the age of 13."

He said, "That's not what I asked you. I said, 'Are you saved?'"

By this time I exploded, "Suppose I am; suppose I'm not. What business is it of yours anyway?"

Do you know what this patient man said? He said, "It's all the business in the world. I've been ordained to preach the gospel to lost creatures."

And I said, "Well, I don't mind you preaching the gospel to lost creatures, but they're in Africa, aren't they? And when you go, let me give you a little advice. Don't use that trite word 'saved.' I mean, that's the word the fanatics use when they pass out pamphlets on street corners."

At this point I expected John Palmer to react violently. But he didn't. Bathed selflessly in the grace of God and anxious to have that grace touch me, he explained what "being saved" really means. He said, "It is a work of God within you. After God reveals to you the fact that you have sinned and fallen short of His glory, you must confess that sin and acknowledge the fact that Christ paid its penalty in full when He died upon the cross. Then by an act of faith you must ask Christ to come and indwell you, bringing His forgiveness for the past and His power for the future. What you are being saved from is not only the eternal separation from God that awaits unconfessed sinners but also the destructive power of your own selfish motives. This is what you are being saved *from*. Now what are you being saved *for*? You are being saved *for* the purpose of glorifying God with your life."

There it was: the answer to "Why was I born?" God loved me so much that He had sent right to my doorstep a man with the answer to my question about life's purpose. But was I ready to make that purpose my own? Not yet. The whole approach was too "evangelistic" for me.

So John tried another approach. He led my husband and me into a detailed study of the Scriptures, using the Westminster Confession and Catechism as guides. It was this beautifully systematic approach to truth that God used to break the back of my pride. In our studies we kept coming back to that fundamental question of all questions: What is the chief end and purpose of man? The answer kept leaping off the page: "The chief end and purpose of man is to glorify God and enjoy Him forever."

As this statement bombarded me week after week, the effect that God intended and the change for which John Palmer was praying began to occur in my soul. Almost without my realizing what was happening, God began to melt my heart. I found myself bowing before His majesty and asking His forgiveness for my wasted life. Then I dedicated what was left of my years to the purpose He had for me, asking Him to use me in spite of myself for whatever glory He might receive.

Almost immediately a change began to occur within me. I found myself loving John Palmer. Even his habits began to endear themselves to me. I also began to notice the effects of what Christians call "conversion." It was not one of those dramatic conversions that one reads about in books, but in its gradual, thorough way it was just as real. God's peace began to flood my soul. So did His tremendous motivation. To be sure, there was a price to be paid. My self-oriented life-style had to go. But, oh, the fulfillment that came in its place! I was absolutely amazed to learn that putting God first satisfied me in a way that I could never be satisfied without Him. Now, after 20 years of developing a relationship with my Lord, I can honestly say that I would not trade that precious fellowship with

Him for anything else in the world. He has provided everything I need. And more, so much more, is still available.

But now, what about you? You too can have a new orientation in life, a new perspective, a new peace, a new purpose. As you behold the Lord in the Scriptures (remember you *must* keep reading the Word), dwell on the price He paid for your redemption. Then take a moment to bow your head in reverence and just receive Him in all of His fullness. As you receive Christ as your Saviour and Lord you will find that you are not receiving a religion. You are not even receiving a statement of faith. You are receiving a Person—a Person with the power to change your life. For Christ in you is your "hope of glory" (Col. 1:27). In other words, you can now actually accomplish what you were created to accomplish. You can now "glorify God and enjoy Him forever." This is the essence of what it means to be "saved."

Study Questions
   1.   What does it mean to "receive Christ"?
   2.   Discuss how "receiving Christ" differs from "getting religion."
   3.   What changes should be evident in the life of someone who has received Christ as his Saviour and Lord?

THREE

Yielding to Him

Having received Christ into our lives, we now have the power to do what we could never do without Him—reflect His glorious righteousness. In fact, there should be no limit to what can be accomplished through us if we are truly yielded to God's purposes. Why then do so many of us seem to fall short of our full potential, settling for mediocrity when there could be excellence? What are we afraid of? Why are we holding back?

Remember these headlines: "Runner breaks four-minute mile"; "Runner takes seven gold medals"; "Skater sweeps all"; "Gymnast receives perfect score"; "Hockey team scrambles to victory"? In every one of these incidents, "ordinary" individuals became EXTRAordinary as they lived up to every ounce of potential within them. Do you think that we as Christians should do any less than these athletes?

I am not suggesting that to be approved of God we all have to be winners or even that we have to be "recognized." The runners in the race of life are not really in competition with one another. They are in competition with themselves. They are expected to yield their bodies to God's supernatural power and let God push them beyond their natural limits. Living the Christian life is not a natural experience. It is a SUPERnatural experience. When we forget this truth, we are in trouble.

Come with me, if you will, to ancient Greece where together we will attend the first Olympic games. We want to observe the archery competition, an event requiring tremendous dexterity. In the particular meet we will be watching there are several contestants waiting in line to try their skill at hitting a distant bull's-eye. We notice that, unlike the archery game we are familiar with, the intended target has only one circle, a very small one at that; so you cannot come close and still receive a score. You either hit the mark or you don't. To us the contest seems impossible.

We watch as the first contestant approaches the designated shooting mat. Just by the way he walks it appears that he is not as serious about this contest as he should be. It would be nice to win, he reasons, but no competition is worth investing one's whole life in training. Therefore he has not put in the required hours of practice. We wonder how he ever qualified for this important event.

Slowly our archer picks up an arrow and places it upon his bow. Taking his proper stance, he aims and then shoots. Into the air the arrow soars, wavering slightly as it approaches the target. Uh oh, it misses—a whole foot wide of the circle.

"*Hamartano*," the judge cries in Greek; in English it means, "You missed the mark."

The second contestant is different from the first. He has spent years training for this event. We know, judging from the intense expression on his face as he approaches the shooting mat, that he wants to hit that target with everything that is within him. Nervously he takes the bow, then places his arrow upon it. He assumes the proper stance, carefully taking his aim. Anxiously we await the outcome.

Suddenly the arrow flies very surely, very swiftly from the start. The audience catches its breath. On the missile streaks, then bam! It stops, landing so close to the bull's-eye that the wood of the shaft appears to nick the outside of the circle. Nobody breathes. What will the judge say to this one? Since it is so very, very close, will he be lenient and call it a perfect shot?

"*Hamartano*," the judge proclaims. "You too missed the mark."

There is a spiritual application in this illustration from the early Greek games. Let hitting the bull's-eye represent the goal of living our lives for God's glory. Now notice how differently we humans react to the challenge of hitting God's mark! Some of us go through life not even knowing that there is a target we are supposed to shoot for. Others of us see the target in the distance, but the task of striking it dead center seems so impossible that we don't bother training too seriously for the competition. Therefore any attempt we make at religiosity comes far short of genuine glory to God.

There are some people, however, who sincerely want to give God all He requires. Therefore they spend a major portion of their lives trying very hard to hit the designated target. They get baptized, go through catechism classes, take communion, attend church regularly, and obey all the rules the church imposes upon them. But even so they fall short of the mark of the glory of God, maybe not by so great a distance as some of their less religious friends, but short enough to be proclaimed a failure by the holy Judge.

You see, it doesn't matter whether we miss God's bull's-eye by a foot or only by a fraction of an inch. The Judge's pronouncement is the same: "*Hamartano*; you missed the mark." As a matter of fact, every human being who has ever lived, no matter how religious he may try to be, receives the same evaluation of his efforts. The Bible says, "For all have sinned and fall short of the glory of God" (Rom. 3:23). The word "sin" then, which in this particular context is the Greek word *hamartano*, is defined more broadly than the usual explanation of transgressing the law of God (although transgression is definitely part of sinning). Rather, "sin" in its all-encompassing definition is missing the mark of God's glory.

If we were to leave the Greek games at this point we would go away with defeat in our memories and discouragement in our hearts. But we would be leaving entirely too soon. Look at that next contestant. Where in the world did he come from? Why didn't we notice him before? How regal he looks in his flowing white robe! With what assurance he approaches the contestant's mat! The tenderness with which he strokes the feathers on the arrow makes us wonder if indeed he fashioned them. With skill he places the arrow on the bow. There! It is perfect. Everything is ready. Now he assumes the proper archer's stance, setting his face like a flint as he concentrates on the target he wants to pierce.

In a flash the arrow is released, cutting the air with precision. We find ourselves catching our breath in unison with the rest of the audience. Every spectator at the competition is pulling for this contestant. You can sense a spirit of oneness as the arrow approaches the target. It seems to be flying perfectly. Indeed it is, for it hits—right on!

The judge rushes over to the target, scrutinizing this latest attempt to hit the mark of God's glory. There is no question in anyone's mind. The arrow has struck dead center.

A hush continues to grip the spectators as they wait for the judge's pronouncement. Deliberately his words cut through the charged anticipation of the moment. "Well done, good and faithful servant. You have hit the mark of God. Many have tried and some have come very close. But only you, out of all the people who have ever competed, have hit the mark right on. Only you have brought God glory with every moment of your existence. Only you have never sinned. Identify yourself, O contestant; and do it loud enough for all the world to hear."

We shift our gaze to the contestant's mat just in time to catch a glimpse of the authoritative figure in white. Planting His feet firmly on the ground beneath Him and folding His hands behind His back, He raises His head and boldly declares, "I am the Christ, the Son of the living God." We fall on our faces in worship.

In my meditation of the moment I picture myself waiting in line to take my turn at trying to hit the bull's-eye. As a contestant in this competition called life, I too must make an attempt to hit the very distant, very difficult mark of God. But I don't know if I have the strength to lift the bow. My knees have turned to water, my heart to a rapidly pounding alarm. How would *you* like to follow a performance like that?

Just as I am about to admit defeat without even taking my shot, the tall stranger in white comes over and puts His arm around my shoulder. Tenderly He looks me in the eye. I feel my heart melting under the warmth of His love. "Would you like me to shoot for you?" He asks.

"Would I?" I reply, considering the question too good to be true. "Would I? You bet I would!"

Thus I take the very first step in reaching my potential for God's glory. I yield my life to Jesus Christ, letting Him do *for* me what I am powerless to do myself. It is an exciting beginning. But it is only a beginning; I will have to "let God do it" any time, any place I want to be truly used for His glory.

Reader, you too are expected to hit the mark of God's glory. And you too will fall short of the bull's-eye. What are you going to do about your failure? Are you going to ignore it? Are you going to let it frustrate you the rest of your years on this earth? Or are you going to give your life to Jesus Christ and let Him do *for* you what you cannot do yourself? Only then will you become everything you were designed to be. Only then will you begin to live unreservedly for the marvelous goal of glorifying God.

Now try to grasp an important truth. Whereas Christ through His *life* can be our helper, teaching us how to shoot properly, and Christ through His *death* can be our substitute, actually doing the shooting in our place, it is Christ through His *resurrection* who becomes our power source, hitting the mark of God through the bodies which He has given us for that purpose.

As we yield our lives to the resurrected Christ to be used as He desires for His glory, God meets us with some exciting promises. He says He will do the exact same things for us that He did for His very own Son. He says He will strengthen us "with might by His Spirit in the inner man" (Eph. 3:16) and reveal to us "the exceeding greatness of His power . . . His mighty power which He worked in Christ when He raised Him from the dead and set Him at His right hand in the heavenly places" (Eph. 1:19,20). For what purpose does He do all this? The answer repeats itself several times in the first chapter of the book of Ephesians: "that we . . . should be to the praise of His glory" (Eph. 1:12).

With our mission in life so designated and our equipment all provided, you would think we'd approach each day with real determination and excitement. But we seem hesitant to let God's strength manifest itself, don't we? Is our problem one of the will? Or is it a matter of fear? If the latter, what are we afraid of? Are we afraid of what might happen if God really *did* release His power through us?

It's time to yield to that power and find out. It's time to let God develop the potential which He has placed within us. It's time to say, "Lord Jesus, I'm yours—all of me. I'm weak. I'm unable. I'm insecure and I'm afraid. I can't hit any target you place before me. But, Lord, I know you can. So help me, dear Jesus; shoot through me."

Then we will discover the liberating truth that where we may fall short of the mark, Jesus Christ hits it right on. Not only does He hit it once but He hits it every time He tries. Such realization should make life exciting for it turns every day into an adventure in glory. And we are privileged to be participants in that adventure. We, the weakest of contestants in this gruelling competition called life, are learning at last that human potential can become God-empowered if that potential is simply yielded to Christ.

Study Questions

1. List as many definitions for sin as you can think of. Which definition is the most all-encompassing?

2. What are some ways that Christ "hit the mark of God's glory" during His earthly ministry?

3. Since Christ's resurrected power indwells those of us who are believers, what are some of the things we should now be able to do—things that would be impossible without that power?

FOUR

Communing with Him

If we want to grow in our new relationship with the Lord, becoming sensitive to how He wants us to glorify Him each day, it is essential that we learn how to commune with Him on a moment-by-moment basis. Actually the word "commune" suggests a mutual exchange between us and the Lord who loves us. It involves both listening to the Lord for what He might want to say to us and then responding to His communication by sharing our thoughts.

There are two types of communion with God. The first we'll call general communion; the second, specific communion. General communion is what Christians are supposed to be involved in every moment of every day. It is an attitude of worship and awe. In contrast, specific communion is not an attitude but an action. It usually consists of Bible reading and prayer performed daily at a designated time. In both cases communion is a two-way interaction between God and man. God speaks and man listens. Then man speaks and God listens.

We'll consider general communion first. It is a receptive attitude to what God is constantly saying. The key to practicing it lies in learning how to listen. God speaks through His creation. But in the hustle and bustle of life, how much do we really hear? Try a little experiment. Some night when the family is tucked securely in bed, sneak outside to some quiet place and just listen for the Lord. Lift your eyes to His velvet sky and catch the whisper of the stars.

Right now man is investing millions of dollars listening to the sounds of the universe. He hopes someday to be able to decipher a cherished message from outer space. Well, it's just possible that you might get one before he does. For those diamonds in the sky, some thousands of light-years away, pulsate repeated messages to earth. Over and over again, the sounds beam hope to the remotest parts of our planet: "God made us, God made us, God made us." "The heavens declare the glory of God; and the firmament sheweth his handiwork" (Ps. 19:1).

You don't have to wait until night, though, to hear God talk to you. He speaks in the daytime too. In the crow of the rooster, the chirp of the cardinal, the rustle of the leaves, the day belches forth divine truth. Always the message is the same: "The hand that made us is the Lord's." Learn to listen for God.

I know listening is hard in the frantic pace in which we live. If you're anything like me, instead of hearing the Lord's voice, you hear everything else *but* that. Life is a cacophony of sound: alarm clocks, telephone calls, traffic whistles, car horns, freight trains, jet planes, and many angry voices. Learning to listen for the voice of God in the midst of all this din takes practice. But it is possible. I know. When I had three children under age three chasing each other through the house, the only way I could keep my sanity was to withdraw to the sanctuary of my communion. Now that the children are teenagers, instead of escaping cops 'n robbers I withdraw from stereos, TVs, and tape decks. But the art I learned in those early years of parenthood is still with me and growing more precious all the time.

Sometimes we create our own commotion. Listening

to the radio or watching television may block any communication the Lord may want to have with us. I am not condemning Christian programming or gospel music, for they are a blessing to a great many people. But even these should be monitored. And as far as soap operas or off-color situation comedies are concerned, not only will they block the airways that the Lord may want to use but they will actually give credence in our lives to the distracting voices of the world.

After Christ came to dwell in my life there were several changes that had to be made and they had to be made quickly if I was going to do any spiritual growing. The most obvious change concerned my attitude toward noise. When I was a teenager I was so addicted to listening to the radio that I would sometimes have it on all through the day and night, even while I was sleeping. I loved the swinging tunes of my era and took pride in being able to name the top 10 on the hit parade anytime anybody asked me.

After I married, my radio continued to blare. It kept me company on the days when I was home alone. In fact, it almost became my god. It was a comforter, a counselor, and a constant companion—everything the Lord should have been in my life. When I became a Christian such idolatry could no longer be tolerated. So one day, when my radio was pounding with rhythm, God spoke. "How in the world can you expect me to get through to you with all that noise constantly jamming the air waves?" He shouted. Although the voice He used was not audible, it was every bit as impressive as if it were.

Astounded at my own insensitivity, I answered, "Lord, I guess you can't. I'm sorry. I just never thought of the possibility that you might want to talk to me, not personally, I mean. I'll turn the radio off. Honestly I will."

I *did* turn the radio off. And I have never turned it back on, not to receive anything except news and weather reports. Furthermore, I have not been sorry. For now God, not the radio, is my Comforter, my Counselor, and my constant Companion. In the quiet of my home I am learning how to practice sweet communion with Him. Sometimes God speaks to me, usually by means of a "still, small voice" deep within my soul. My problem now is not in hearing Him. My problem now is in obeying Him. That is the harder task. But my obedience is made easier by the precious fellowship that we have with each other. Most of the time the Lord and I just relish the enjoyment of being together. In fact, there are times when we feel so much at home with each other that there really is no need to say anything. We commune silently, thoroughly, and quite effectually.

A word of caution may be in order here. I am not suggesting that we all become so "spaced out" that when someone talks to us, we jump. When God says, "Pray without ceasing" (1 Thess. 5:17) He means, "Be in an attitude of prayer all the time." Pray when you're driving to and from work. Pray when you're vacuuming. Pray when you're gardening. Pray in the office, the kitchen, the car. Practice God's presence everywhere. But don't lose your grip on reality.

Throw out your misconceptions about prayer. You don't have to pray with your eyes shut. On the freeway that would be disastrous. Take a lesson from the Lord. In the Garden of Gethsemane He "lifted up His eyes to heaven" and prayed magnificently to the Father (John 17:1). You don't have to be on your knees either. Christians pray standing, sitting, and prostrate on their faces. It is the communion that matters, not the posture.

Praying continually does not mean that you repeat the "Our Father" over and over again. What it does mean is that you develop an ear that listens and a heart that responds. The response does not have to be formal. A

"Praise the Lord!" will do. Or "Help me!" if you're in trouble. Or "I love you, Father" if your heart is overflowing. It is a matter of learning how to react to the evidence of God's presence which is constantly manifesting itself all around you.

In addition to general communion with God there should be a time reserved each day for planned, specific communion. Either one without the other is incomplete. If you say, "I commune with God all the time; I don't need to have personal devotions," you are missing a great blessing in your life. If, on the other hand, you say, "I've had my devotions for the day; now I can forget about God," you are cutting yourself off from the dynamic fellowship that can be yours on a moment-by-moment basis.

In order to hold personal devotions, you don't have to wait for God to initiate a conversation with you. He has already done that in His Word. If you want to know what God is saying to you today, just sit down and open your Bible. It doesn't matter whether you turn to Genesis or Revelation, you will find a timely message. Once you receive that message you will want to reply in prayer. The time you set aside for this interchange of ideas doesn't have to be long, but it definitely should be regular. Make an appointment with God and keep it as diligently as you would keep any other important engagement.

Choose whichever time of day suits you best. If you are a morning person, perhaps you should "gather your manna" before anyone else is up. Then you will have the proper food to carry you through the rest of the day. For you a guiding Scripture verse is, "My voice shalt thou hear in the morning, O Lord; in the morning will I direct my prayer unto thee" (Ps. 5:3).

If you are more awake in the evening than you are in the morning, let God have *that* time of day. He deserves your best, whenever it is. The danger in waiting too long, though, is that by the time you get to it other things may have crowded out your devotional time. Then if you get it in at all it runs the risk of being rushed.

Personally, I prefer noon. By then my routine necessities are out of the way and I'm ready for a treat from the Lord. I once counseled a woman who, in tears, asked me to help her get her devotional life in order.

"What's the matter?" I asked, trying to guess the nature of the problem. "Are you having trouble fitting your devotions into the day?"

"Oh, no," she exclaimed, "that's not it at all. It's my housework I can't fit into the day. I open my Bible the minute the kids leave for school. Then I get so involved in what I'm reading that it's often lunchtime before I realize it. My husband gets upset when the house isn't straightened up by the time he gets home from work. And I get upset because *he's* upset. Can you help me get organized?"

My advice was simple. "Do what I do. Practice general communion from the moment you get up. But save your specific communion until you finish your housework. Then your devotional time will be a reward, not a problem." The woman accepted the advice, organized her day, and turned into a productive Christian at peace with her husband, with herself, and with God.

Take a moment to examine your own devotional life. Are you having trouble with it? Then maybe the hour you're holding it (or *think* you should be holding it) is not right for you. Try fitting it into a different spot on your schedule. Remember God is more flexible than you are. He'll grant you an appointment anytime, day or night. But once the appointment time is set, He does expect you to keep it.

Communing with God is a thrilling privilege. It should be the desire of every Christian who wants to know more of his Lord. Whether he practices general communion during the hubbub of busyness or specific communion in the sanctuary of a moment, there must be the total experience of listening for God to speak and the response of a heart that has heard His message. The Bible says, "Seek the Lord and his strength, seek his face continually. . . . Give unto the Lord the glory due unto his name: . . . worship the Lord in the beauty of holiness" (1 Chron. 16:11,29). Such worship lays the most solid foundation I can think of for glorifying God and actually enjoying Him—not occasionally, not even frequently, but moment by precious moment.

Study Questions

    1. Define "communion with God."

    2. What are some of the hindrances to effective communion with the Lord?

    3. Suggest how to remove these hindrances or, if that is impossible, to work around them and still commune.

FIVE

Becoming His Channel

Once we have learned how to commune properly, then we are ready to be used. I like to think of Christians as conduits for conveying God's blessings to others. At one end of the conduit there is a tremendous source of power and at the other, dry, thirsty land. It is God's desire to gush through us with His rivers of living water to quench the thirst at the other end of the pipe. If, however, our pipes are clogged, God's power can't get through. Therefore it is essential that confession become part of our communion.

In fact, confession of sin is really the first step in any meaningful relationship with God, whether that relationship be an initial one or one that is being restored after a painful breach of fellowship. The second step is presenting our vessels, now cleansed, to God to be used as He sees fit. The Bible tells us to "come boldly to the throne of grace, that we may obtain mercy and find grace to help in time of need" (Heb. 4:16). A bold entrance into the heavenly holy of holies would be unthinkable, however, if it were not for Jesus Christ, the One who has opened the door. The Scripture says that "we have a great High Priest who has passed through the heavens, Jesus the Son of God," who can be touched with the feeling of our infirmities because He "was in all points tempted as we are, yet without sin" (Heb. 4:14,15). This High Priest has granted us access into the very presence of God.

As most of us know, the Hebrew Tabernacle is an Old Testament picture of salvation. God, in His Shekinah glory, used to enclose Himself in a very secluded part of the structure called the holy of holies. This sanctuary, which contained the Ten Commandments and the mercy seat, was shut off from the rest of the Tabernacle by a very heavy drapery called "the vail." Only the high priest was allowed to enter through the vail and then only once a year. When he did enter he had to be totally pure, clean both physically and spiritually. Carrying the blood of a sacrificial lamb to sprinkle upon the mercy seat, he approached God's presence very cautiously. His life was hanging in the balance.

If the high priest accomplished his task according to divine instructions, the Lord accepted the sacrifice and covered the sins of disobedient Israel, at least for another year. The priest then emerged from the sanctuary one happy man. And the anxious congregation openly expressed relief at having escaped the judgment of a wrathful God.

If something went wrong with the sacrificial procedure, however, the priest was struck dead by the finger of God and the people were left waiting, without any covering for their sin. Clearly a more perfect means of atonement was needed. And that means was provided in Jesus Christ.

Assuming the role of high priest, "He entered the Most Holy Place once for all, having obtained eternal redemption" for us (Heb. 9:12). The cross was His mercy seat; the blood of the lamb, His own blood. "It is finished," the Lord proclaimed when atonement for sin was complete. Then to show us that the Father had accepted the sacrifice, the vail in the temple was "torn in two" (Matt. 27:51).

What a marvelous act of mercy! Now you and I, without the help of any earthly priest, can enter God's presence at any time through the blood of the Father's own

Lamb, Jesus Christ. But what does all of this talk about the Tabernacle have to do with the subject of this book? Just this: since the glory of God abides in the holy of holies our only access to that glory is to pass through the torn "vail," the finished work of Christ on the cross.

So through Christ we enter into the glory of God's presence. Then what? How does God's presence pass through us to others? The answer is basic: in the form of God's free-flowing Word. You see, if we take in so much of the Scriptures that we can't hold any more inside us, then God's truth has no place else to go but out—out through us into the lives of others.

It will also flow up, up to the throne of God. When we become so filled with the words of the Lord, it is natural to respond with words of our own. This verbal response is what we call prayer. As we have already noted, true fellowship is, of necessity, a two-way, not a one-way, communication. God communes with us through the Bible and we communicate with Him through prayer. If we are reading the Word of God daily, then our prayers to Him should be what the Bible calls "effectual"—producing the effect intended. If our prayers are effectual He will answer them. And through the answers God will be glorified.

So then, if our chief end and purpose is to glorify the Lord who made us, there is no more meaningful way of doing so than to yield ourselves to His power through prayer. This call to yield, however, brings up another question. What is prayer anyway? Is it something that we initiate and then get frustrated with because God doesn't answer our way? Or is it something God initiates to which we actively respond? There is a popular slogan that reads, "Prayer changes things." Well, it does, but only from our point of view. From God's point of view, "Prayer accomplishes things," for God's plan never changes; it is only carried out.

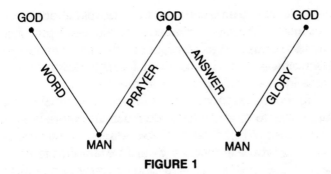

FIGURE 1

Notice in Figure 1 we have formed the letter *W*—a letter which we will let stand for our proper worship of God. Notice also that of the five points it takes to form this *W*, the top three represent God and the bottom two represent man. The *W* takes shape when the five points are connected. Through His Word God initiates prayer, the true kind of prayer that produces holy results. "Word," in this case, can be any communication of God to man, any "burdening" communication, that is. God burdens us to pray about things He wants to see happen on earth. Sensitive Christians feel the Lord's burden and pray for His power to be released in order to accomplish His purposes. Then God answers our requests because He has burdened us to make those requests in the first place. Having received our answer, we then respond in praise. The *W* has been completed. We are gratified and God is glorified. This is a picture of exciting communion, right in the center of God's perfect will. There is no room for frustration in this kind of praying. And there is no room for "unanswered" prayer.

Sometimes, however, instead of letting God initiate prayer, we try to initiate it ourselves. We start at the second point of the *W* and end at the third or fourth—an inverted *V*. God is not usually glorified through such petitions. And if any answers do come our way, they are apt to bounce back to us in very unusual ways. For example, shortly after I became a Christian, I prayed a self-initiated prayer. I wanted to be used as a witness but I didn't know how to go about witnessing. So I said, "Lord, I want to share my faith today. Please send a lost soul to my doorstep."

My motive was good. There's no question about that. But I forgot to listen for God's instructions before I made my request. If I had read the Scriptures in any one of several appropriate places I would have seen the command, "Go." Instead, I asked God to do *for* me what He had instructed me to do myself; namely, put myself in contact with someone in need of salvation.

Almost as soon as the prayer was out of my mouth I realized how ridiculous it was, especially since New England, where we were living at the time, was having one of the worst blizzards of its history. Not a soul was moving on the street. The milkman couldn't even get through the drifts. As the snowstorm worsened I started making excuses for God.

"Lord," I prayed, "you can send somebody tomorrow if you want to. I mean, today is awfully stormy."

The Lord was not about to be intimidated by a brash new Christian. Right after lunch the doorbell rang. I couldn't believe my ears. I dropped my dustcloth and opened the door. There she was: my poor lost soul. She was "collecting for a charity," she said—in one of the worst blizzards I had ever seen.

Well, if God was going to go to all this trouble to bring somebody to my door, I knew I had to keep my part of the bargain. I shared my faith with the lady. Amazingly, she wasn't turned off. After I finished witnessing and had given her a donation for her charity I dismissed her politely and resumed my housework. For the rest of the day I praised the Lord for my marvelous answer to prayer.

The answer was so great, in fact, I decided to try it again. The next day I got up and offered the Lord my same self-initiated prayer. Right after lunch the doorbell rang again. This time I didn't even drop my dustcloth. I opened the door dustcloth in hand, wondering who would be in need of a witness today. When I saw her face, my mouth must have dropped to my knees. For there in front of me was the same woman I had shared with yesterday. She had come again. In fact, she came every day that week and continued to come every day for months. She didn't stop coming until long after I ceased offering my very immature prayer.

God was teaching me a lesson. He knew it and so did I. Think of all of the hours of my time that woman consumed! And she never came to a saving knowledge of my Lord. Furthermore, she definitely hindered me from reaching out to someone more responsive.

I've learned some things about prayer since then and am continuing to learn more every day. The most valuable lesson God is trying to teach me, I think, is to listen before I respond, to read the Word before I make a request.

Since I've shared with you an example of the "inverted V" type of praying, let me also share an example of prayer as part of God's perfect W. In this case Moses is the one who offered the petition. I'm sure you will see right away that he did much better than I. The background of his prayer is this: Moses was up on Mount Sinai with God, receiving the Ten Commandments and experiencing sweet communion with his Lord. When he didn't return to his people as quickly as they thought he should, they became restless and decided to make an idol. So with their melted jewelry they fashioned a golden calf, built an altar before it, and offered burnt offerings and peace offerings.

This blasphemy made the Lord so angry that He

threatened to destroy the whole nation of Israel. He said to Moses, "Now therefore let me alone, that my wrath may wax hot against them, and that I may consume them: and I will make of thee a great nation" (Exod. 32:10).

If Moses had not just been face to face with the manifest glory of God he might have been tempted to pray amiss. Here God was, offering to create a new nation out of Moses' own loins instead of continuing with the nation created out of the loins of Abraham. Why, Moses could have become the ancestor of God-honoring millions!

But Moses was not tempted. His life had been dedicated to a purpose greater than bringing glory to himself. Therefore, "Moses besought the Lord" (Exod. 32:11), reminding God of His mighty acts on behalf of the children of Israel. He also suggested that God's great glory might be dimmed in the eyes of the Egyptians if He, who had granted such miraculous deliverance, should suddenly turn on these whom He had freed to "consume them from the face of the earth." Therefore, Moses pleaded, "Turn from thy fierce wrath, and repent of this evil against thy people" (Exod. 32:12).

I strongly believe that God had burdened Moses to pray this prayer, that Moses' intercession was God's decreed means of carrying out His original purpose for Israel. "How," you might ask, "did Moses know what was expected of him?" Well, when he came down from that mountain after having beheld the glory of the Lord, he was carrying close to his heart the tablets bearing God's instructions for his life. Besides that he had tucked into his memory God's promise to Abraham. It is God's Word, you remember, that sets into motion effectual prayer.

Moses took that Word and offered it back up to God. He said, "Remember, Lord, you said. . ." (what an effective way to pray!). "Remember, Lord, you said to Abraham, 'I will multiply your seed as the stars of heaven, and all this land that I have spoken of will I give unto your seed, and they shall inherit it for *ever*'" (*see* Exod. 32:13).

What was God supposed to do? Here was His servant tossing His own words back up to Him with boldness that can only come from being in the center of God's will. God responded appropriately. The Bible says, "And the Lord repented of the evil which he thought to do unto his people" (Exod. 32:14). He did not consume the nation Israel.

What really happened in this instance? Did God change from plan A to plan B and then back to plan A again? No. As I see it, plan A was always in motion. But God chose to accomplish it through Moses' prayer. In other words, God gave Moses His Word, Moses prayed that Word back to God, God honored the prayer, and God's original plan was carried out. But it was carried out *through* man's intercession rather than *in spite of* it. God does not *have* to move through men, but He does. And when He does, what a marvelous privilege He affords us to manifest His glory through the exciting channel of prayer!

Other extraordinary answers have come through effectual prayer. Abraham prayed and became a father at the ripe old age of 100. Joshua prayed and the sun stood still. Gideon prayed and managed to defeat a host of the enemy with only a handful of men.

Prayer is powerful. We all know that. But there is a tendency to read this list of great happenings and say, "Well, those were all extraordinary men. Extraordinary men receive extraordinary answers from God. I'm just an ordinary person. So all I can expect from the Lord are just ordinary answers to prayer."

You are absolutely wrong. Every one of these men had very ordinary problems. Abraham lied on occasion. Joshua wasn't sure he could be a leader on his own.

Gideon didn't trust the Lord until he had a sign. And as far as Moses is concerned, he felt totally inadequate for the task to which God was obviously calling him. Each of these men had problems that all of us face. Yet each of them knew how to lay hold of the power of God.

That same power is available to us today. But it must be tapped God's way. We must approach the Lord in the manner prescribed by Him: with confession on our lips, with Christ in our hearts, and with the holy Scriptures tucked inside our souls. Then we can offer our petitions to the Lord and expect Him to answer according to the manner in which we have prayed. If we have prayed effectually, the right answer will be forthcoming and God will be glorified through it. The W will have been completed through us. Just think. If this happens, not only will we have established sweet communion with our Lord but we will be in a position where God can really use us as channels to accomplish His purposes; use us to manifest His glory.

Study Questions

1. What does "effectual prayer" consist of?

2. Name some biblical personalities who prayed effectually.

3. What made their prayers effectual?

PART II

A Proper Attitude
Toward Myself

SIX

Offering My Weaknesses

So far we have established the fact that in order to live lives that radiate the Lord's glory, we need to have a right orientation toward God. Now we will see that it is also important to develop a right attitude toward ourselves. After all, we are the ones God has chosen to use.

Come with me to a good old-fashioned New England flea market and listen to some of the remarks that are being made:

"Look at this Paul Revere bowl! Handmade by the silversmith himself."

"Come here and see this old rolling pin. My mom used to have one of these."

"I wonder how this old plate got chipped. Maybe it was hurriedly packed away as soldiers were pounding on the door."

Flea markets are interesting places, aren't they? Some of the values are really surprising. Do you notice that the older the object is, the more it seems to be worth? Do you realize that this handmade artifact I am holding, even with its obvious irregularities, will command a much higher price than its perfect, machine-made counterpart? Look at those buyers searching for cracks or chips to authenticate their purchases. How wise they are—much smarter than the ordinary public!

What a spiritual lesson there is for Christians in the

seeming worthlessness of the flea market! For in the topsy-turvy value system of life, vessels for which the world pays millions cannot be used by God at all—not until they are broken. On the other hand, vessels which the world discards are often the very ones the Lord considers to be the most precious treasures of all.

Unfortunately, we tend to pay more attention to the world's way of looking at value than we do to the Lord's. Listen to the clay talking back to the Potter:

"I'm too old. Let me sit on the shelf."

"I've got a physical defect. God would never want me."

"I'm not attractive enough."

"I don't have any talent."

"I'm scared to death to get up in front of people."

Such are the excuses we offer to God. Shame on us! We sound as if the way we turned out is a surprise to the Potter who made us. I am certainly thankful that God ignores such nonsense. I am also thankful that He assures us again and again that He has chosen us just as we are, that He has chosen us to be filled with Himself and His glory. In fact, for this awesome task He has purposely selected the least of us—vessels of clay, fragile vessels that sometimes break, vessels with cracks, vessels with flaws. Why? We go to the Bible for the answer. It says, "We have this treasure in earthen vessels, that the excellence of the power may be of God and not of us" (2 Cor. 4:7).

You see, if our outer appearance was perfect it might detract from the glory within. If we did everything flawlessly we, not the Lord, might receive the praise. But if, on the other hand, we stumble and fail yet find ourselves being used anyway, then there's only one place for the glory to go, and that's directly to Him.

God is saying to you and me today, "Dear believer, give me your weakness. Don't you know that weakness is what I use best? It's not your abilities, your self-confidence, your self-assurance that I want (although I can move through all of those things). Rather, it's your inabilities, your fears, and your shortcomings that give me the greatest opportunity to be God. So go ahead and say, 'I can't.' Those words are your gateway to victory. For I intend to take them and infuse them with my strength, my power, and my might. What you can't do, I can. Where you fail, I will succeed. Where you falter, I will rise in power. My glory *will* be manifest in you."

Sometimes we end up being better instruments in God's service in areas where we feel ill-equipped than in areas where we are sure of ourselves. I am a living example of this phenomenon. Having been reared on a farm where the closest neighbor was a healthy jaunt across the fields, I developed into a quiet, reticent, stick-close-to-Mommy lass, who had very few friends and even less self-confidence. Whenever a grown-up would try to befriend me, I would dive into Mother's skirts and silently pray to become invisible. It never worked.

Having to go to school was traumatic. I got through my kindergarten year on lettuce sandwiches because that was all my churning tummy could handle. Sometimes I even had trouble with those. Then Mommy would come and rescue me and take me home to the farm. There I discovered my tummy could handle anything.

Somehow I managed to get through all nine elementary school years, but I did so without ever raising my hand to volunteer any thoughts or comments. I spoke only when the teacher directly addressed me. "Peggy is quiet," the report card would read. That was the understatement of the decade.

Then came the challenge of high school. I was beginning to emerge from my shell and to enjoy the world around me. Those four years of learning and social interaction with friends bring back sweet memories of victory—victory in every area except one, that is. I was required to take a mini-course in speech. I recall the ordeal with horror. One day all the students in the class were expected to give a three-minute discourse on a subject which the teacher had handed out only a couple of minutes before. I took one look at my topic, could think of only one sentence to say, rattled off that sentence three times, and sat down. I had failed.

That frustrating experience so terrified me that by the time I got to college, I avoided public speaking altogether. Believe it or not, I graduated with a respectable degree in English without ever having had one course in speech.

Then I became a Christian. God said, "Yield me your life." I did so. That is, I yielded all of my life except the area of public speaking. I said, "God, you may use me in any way you want to, but PLEASE don't make me speak."

God replied, "Sorry. A speaker you are going to be."

I froze. "Lord, you've got to be kidding. Why would you choose my weakness?"

He answered, "Because I don't want you to get in my way. If I choose your area of need, you won't be launching out on your own. You will HAVE to come to me because you won't be able to do the job without me. I want you constantly dependent and yielded."

That thought exchange took place almost 20 years ago, but I am still learning the fine art of yielding. You may be wondering why the art of public speaking would be difficult to someone trained and experienced in public school teaching. I am not sure of the answer to that question except to say that to me there is a tremendous difference between teaching a class of students and giving an inspirational message at a banquet. During teaching, the students' eyes are usually riveted either on the blackboard, on their notebooks, or on their texts. During a speech, those same eyes rarely leave the speaker. At first I found this prospect terrifying. At times I became nauseous just thinking about it. But when God said "Go!" I walked to the speaker's platform. I've been walking there ever since.

I dearly love teaching and have been involved in explaining truths to somebody or other for most of my adult life. Whenever I can turn a speaking engagement into a teaching session from the Bible, I do so and really enjoy it. But there are always those banquet-type affairs where nobody in the audience has a "textbook." Then the butterflies come.

Actually, God has me right where He wants me. He knows I have nothing within myself to give. Everything *has* to come from Him. Time and time again He proves His sufficiency. Often just when I feel the weakest, the Holy Spirit will choose to sweep through my body in power. Sometimes I can actually feel the electricity of His presence. When that happens, lives are changed for His glory. I do nothing but stand there and marvel.

"O the depth of the riches both of the wisdom and knowledge of God! How unsearchable are His judgments and His ways past finding out!" (Rom. 11:33). The longer a believer trusts the Lord, the more he appreciates the truth of these words. God's ways really *are* past finding out, aren't they? Wise human investors may know how to turn the discarded artifacts of a flea market into objects of recognized value, but who except God would choose a seemingly worthless human vessel and use it to manifest glory? Who but God would take a weakness and change it into strength? Nobody. But God does and does it well.

Consider the Lord's explanation for vessels He has chosen to use: "Not many wise according to the flesh, not many mighty, not many noble, are called. But God has chosen the foolish things of the world to put to shame the wise, and God has chosen the weak things of the world to put to shame the things which are mighty; and the base things of the world and things which are despised God has chosen, and the things which are not, to bring to nothing the things that are, that no flesh should glory in His presence" (1 Cor. 1:26-29).

Let the impact of these words really sink in. God is saying that He has deliberately selected for service the foolish, the weak, the base, the despised, and the nothings. Furthermore, He says He has done so in order that no one can rob Him of His glory. Not one of us is left out of His plan. And not one of us will fall short of fulfilling it if we will simply yield to His hand.

Filled with inabilities and insecurities, bent on sinning but trying to grow in grace, Christians through the centuries have upended the world with God's power. Now it's our turn to do the same thing. You ask, How can weak vessels like us accomplish such a feat? The answer is, The same way the early disciples accomplished it. As we have seen, by yielding our weaknesses to the Lord, we tap His reservoir of strength.

So next time you are tempted to say, "God can never use me," remember *you* are the vessel Christ paid to redeem. When He sweat drops of blood in the garden, it was you for whom He was planning to die. When He cried on the cross in great agony, it was your place in hell He was taking. When He entered God's presence in glory, it was to prepare a mansion just for you. And when He invaded your life in the person of His Spirit, He was singling you out for His service. Now let Him use you in the way He has planned (which might, by the way, differ from your plans). Let Him move through your weaknesses, your reticence, your fears. Allow Him to make you into a vessel that can visibly radiate His glory.

Study Questions

1. Why do you think God allows us to have weaknesses?

2. Are there times in our lives when our weaknesses can actually be beneficial to us? to others? to God? Explain

3. Relate some personal experiences in which God's strength has overpowered your weaknesses.

SEVEN

Concentrating on the Spiritual

Having been reminded that God loves to use our weaknesses, we still have to admit that those weaknesses really get to us sometimes, especially the physical ones. Tell me, when you look at your reflection in the mirror each morning, how do you react? Do you feel discouraged? Frustrated? Defeated? Old Father Time has a way of catching up with us, doesn't he?

We women try to cheat him in every way we can possibly think of. We color our hair, blush up our cheeks, moisturize our wrinkles, and camouflage the circles under our eyes. We buy bras that "lift and separate" and girdles that keep supporting us for up to 18 hours a day. Then we put on the most fashionable outfit we can find.

You men are not without your moments of vanity either. I have observed how tenderly you pamper your hair with your stylized razor cuts, your super-curly permanents, your special color formulas, and your expensive and painful transplants—all for a better appearance.

Be that as it may, when we all get our good points accentuated and our faults either covered or deemphasized, we feel good. We have reversed the effects of time—or at least that's what we kid ourselves into thinking. Actually after investing hundreds of dollars in cosmetics and spending countless hours applying them, we feel that we deserve a measure of success.

If any of you ladies happen to live in a house with all men, as I do, you have probably discovered the fact that it doesn't matter too much what you wear. Anything you throw on makes you the prettiest thing around. There isn't any competition anywhere. Most of us women, however, dress for circles that reach beyond our homes. And we meet that challenge quite admirably. When we do a particularly good job of grooming and then enter a roomful of people, it is not unusual for us to receive a compliment. "Doesn't she look lovely?" the voices whisper. We smile with approval at the comment.

It makes us feel like winners, temporarily anyhow. But just when we are beginning really to savor the victory, Father Time starts wagging his tongue. "Tomorrow it's going to be harder to cover the gray in your hair," he taunts. "Tomorrow it's going to be harder to erase the wrinkles in your brow. Tomorrow it's going to be harder to control the bulges in your figure." His singsong voice drones on . . .

Something within us wants to yell, "Be still!" But deep down inside we know he's right. We can see all too clearly a future scene in which we are the center of attention. It is only a figment of our thoughts, to be sure, but one with power to haunt us. In all probability, you see, the scene will become reality. Let me share it.

I invite you to enter a very proper room. Imagine, if you can, a coldly formal setting. Do you recognize the hymns being played on the organ? Smell the lilies. Aren't they pungent? Now notice the open box in the alcove. Ornate, isn't it, with its lining of satin and handles of brass? Is that a person inside? Who do you suppose it is? Why, it's me! I can't believe it. It's me! And I'm dressed in my very finest outfit. It appears that the cosmeticians have been working really hard, but this time their creams are much thicker, this time they had to use deeper colors. For now they are trying to cover the effects of death.

I watch as my friends file slowly by, the way they are expected to do in such situations. I see them mouthing an appropriate cliché: "Doesn't she look lovely?" Only this time the words echo emptiness. Oh, those gals probably just want to say the right thing, the way they have always done in the past. But for some reason the ruse isn't working, not here in front of the satin-draped casket. I am dead. Irrevocably dead. And I cannot scream back my frustration.

How did we humans get caught in such a depressing predicament—in the vise of aging, I mean? Well, the problem began quite subtly long ago in the midst of God's perfect creation. (If you don't mind, I would like to tell the story from the woman's point of view because that's how I, a woman, see it.) When God made woman from the rib of man, He was crowning His delicate handiwork with the most beautiful creation of all. Eve was stunning, vibrantly alive and exciting, and eager to get busy experiencing life.

As the Creator talked over the meaning of existence with Eve, most certainly He revealed her chief end and purpose for living. "I have made you to glorify me," He surely said. And Eve was content to obey—for a little while, at least. Then one day she decided to pursue the desires of her own heart instead of the desires of her Maker.

The consequences of her rebellion came quickly. She noticed the spiritual changes first. Her fellowship with God had been severed. Confusion of purpose plagued her. Self-fulfillment was rapidly becoming her new criterion for making decisions. No longer was her chief end and purpose to glorify God and enjoy Him forever.

This loss of spiritual aim caused physical repercussions as well. But the physical changes took longer to make their presence known. At first, when Eve caught her reflection in the water, her image seemed every bit as lovely as it always had been. This deception led her to believe that she had gotten away with her transgression, physically at least. Just to make sure, though, she checked her appearance daily, hoping that she would *not* see reflected in the pool any indication of physical deterioration.

Then one day it happened. As she was combing her gorgeous hair a strand came out that was a different color from the rest. "What is this?" she must have asked in utter astonishment. "Is this a gray hair? And this furrow in my brow. Is this a wrinkle? Am I aging? Am I going to die? Oh, God, please, don't tell me you meant it when you said, 'the soul that sinneth, it shall die' " (Ezek. 18:20).

Yes, God meant it. In fact, Eve had already died on the inside when her soul was alienated from her Maker. But a change was also beginning to manifest itself on the outside in what we call the aging process.

By now the effect of Eve's sin (which, incidentally, was passed on to Adam and through Adam to us) has reached "the third and fourth generation" and way beyond. It is touching every man and woman alive with its finger of spiritual and physical degeneration. And all because man has rebelled against the reason God gave him for living out his years. "The wages of sin is death" (Rom. 6:23), the Bible says; and sin, you remember, is the state of falling short of God's glory (see Rom. 3:23). Therefore it is possible to conclude that man is both spiritually dead and physically in the process of dying because of his disobedience to God's purposes for his life.

Through practice we ladies are becoming quite good at laughing at our predicament. We shrug our shoulders and say, "Well, every plum *does* become a prune, you know, and every grape a raisin." When the prune or raisin turns out to be us, however, that's a problem that demands some action! So we rush to the nearest drugstore, load up on the best moisturizing agents available, and apply them faithfully to our shriveling skin. But nothing seems to work for very long. We certainly are in need of a better remedy for wrinkles than the short-lived camouflage of cosmetics.

Well, praise the Lord, in Christ we have it. He imparts a gift called the "new birth" that enables its recipients to start life all over again, this time aware of God's purpose. The immediate effects are mainly spiritual but they do touch the physical as well. When we receive Jesus Christ as our Saviour and Lord we begin to experience a quality of life that gets better each day. Along with that life comes a promise that someday our corruptible bodies will rise from the grave in incorruption. But that seems pretty far off, doesn't it? What about our aging bodies NOW?

They too are cared for in a most magnificent way. God says, "Though our outward man is perishing, yet the inward man is being renewed day by day" (2 Cor. 4:16). This is one of my favorite verses because it contrasts what I see happening on the outside with what I cannot see happening on the inside (physically speaking). Truly the ad is correct in saying, "You're not getting older, you're getting better." I *am* getting better—spiritually.

This verse is also my answer to everyone who asks me, "How can I look young at *my* age?" You can take years off your appearance at *any* age by delving into God's Word where the secrets for vibrant living are located. I firmly believe that if we concentrate more on renewing our inner image (the spiritual one), the spiritual change that occurs on the inside will manifest itself physically on the outside. We will benefit in both areas at the same time.

As we begin to comprehend God's marvelous plan for our lives, we will see that each day brings us closer to eternity, not to death and the grave but beyond to eternal life with the Lord. This shift in emphasis from self to God should, in turn, make a difference in our physical appearance. God's peace will start smoothing out our wrinkles. His joy will add a sparkle to our eyes. His guidance will put new purpose in our walk. And His assurance will set us free from stress and tension. Whatever age we find ourselves enjoying, we will always be "young at heart"—or maybe I should say "young at soul."

The key to experiencing everlasting vitality, then, is receiving and reflecting Jesus Christ. I am thoroughly convinced that if Christ is resident within, the evidence will clearly be seen. We will be aglow with the radiance of His glory, living for the same purposes which motivated Him.

Mirrors are God's tools to show us how we are doing. Just as we need a full-length mirror to check on our physical appearance, equally often we need a full-length mirror to check on our spiritual appearance. That mirror is the Word of God. Read it carefully. You will find it filled with practical suggestions for reflecting the glory of God. As you read, take a long, hard look at yourself, starting at the top of your head and proceeding to the tip of your toes.

First examine your eyes. Are they focusing properly today? On what? On yourself, on things, or on Him? Next look at your ears. How well are they hearing right now? Are they tuned to the voices of the world or to what God might be saying to you? What is the shape of your mouth today? Is it crooked with gossip and slander or curved upward in an edifying smile? Are your hands reaching out in mercy? Are your feet shod for sharing the gospel? And what about your knees? Do they show that you have been much in prayer? If not, why not? Are you really reflecting the image of Christ, an image that radiates *His* glory?

The Bible says, "Be doers of the word, and not hearers only, deceiving yourselves. For if anyone is a hearer of the word and not a doer, he is like a man observing his natural face in a mirror; for he observes himself, goes away, and immediately forgets what kind of man he was. But he who looks into the perfect law of liberty and continues in it, and is not a forgetful hearer but a doer of the word, this one will be blessed in what he does" (Jas. 1:22-25).

The Christian who looks into the Scriptures, sees his imperfections, then sets about working on them is indeed blessed of God. For mirrors show not only areas of need, they show areas of improvement as well. They show progress being wrought in lives. And that's exciting. I am told that as I behold "in a mirror the glory of the Lord," I will find myself being changed into that same image. The change will occur gradually ("from glory to glory") and quite supernaturally ("just as by the Spirit of the Lord," 2 Cor. 3:18). But it *will* occur if I keep my eyes in the right place.

If I dwell on my physical regress I will be in a state of constant apprehension. If, on the other hand, I dwell on my spiritual progress I will be filled with contentment and peace. I will be keeping a proper perspective on my life—a perspective that is absolutely necessary if I am to reflect the glory of my Lord and enjoy doing it.

Study Questions

1. What is God's compensation for the process of aging and eventual death?

2. How can we make the most of this compensation?

3. Does spiritual rebirth have any physical effects? If so, what are they?

EIGHT

Appreciating My Worth

As we focus on the fact that we are God's choice to reflect His glorious image on this earth, we should begin to develop a healthy respect for how much we are really worth. Let me illustrate how high a price tag each of us actually bears.

Have you ever browsed in an exclusive dress salon, the kind that sells designer originals? Personally I feel nervous in such places. Everything looks so "rich." Browsing in "rich" boutiques is frustrating for me because I know I won't be able to afford anything on the racks, not unless it's been marked down three or four times, that is. I'm always looking for bargains.

If you should ever work up enough nerve to enter such an establishment, make sure you examine at least one designer original. You will be amazed at what you discover. Why, originals are basically like any other dresses! They have openings for your neck, holes for both of your arms, and a way to get in and out of the garment. Every dress in my closet boasts such features.

But that's where the similarity stops. The price tags are astronomical. The cost is justified, the salesgirl explains, because instead of being mass-produced like their more reasonable counterparts, these garments are cut and fashioned individually. If you should decide to buy one, she continues, you will become the proud owner of a unique creation, a one-of-a-kind in the fashion world. Supposedly this precaution will keep you from seeing yourself coming and going in the office, in the mall, or at a party.

While you are examining the garment, peek at either the back of the neck or at the side seam about halfway down. See the label? Isn't it impressive? It bears the signature of the designer himself! If you wear this garment well you should be a credit not only to the one who created it but also to yourself. So be prepared for a generous share of compliments.

What a spiritual lesson there is in this analogy of garments! Did you know that you and I are God's designer originals? Like dresses, all of us have many similarities to one another. We have eyes, ears, noses, legs, arms, and heads. But that's where our similarities stop. Each of us has been individually fashioned by the Great Designer Himself. Of the billions of people He has made, no two are exactly alike. Isn't that a staggering thought? Even those of us who are parents of identical twins notice how dissimilar their personalities are.

Since God has made each of us different, He intends to use each of us differently to glorify His name. Therefore to strive for conformity is wrong, especially in spiritual matters. Just as our design is individual, so is God's pattern for our lives. It is wise then not to covet someone else's natural talent or someone else's spiritual gift or even someone else's experience with the Lord. Each of us is unique in God's sight and should thoroughly enjoy that uniqueness.

Now look for your Designer's name. You'll see it written everywhere. Also take a peek at your price tag. It is clear that no earthly purchaser can afford you. But a heavenly purchaser can—and did—when He laid down His life on a cross. You were bought at great sacrifice, "not

. . . with corruptible things, like silver or gold, . . . but with the precious blood of Christ" (1 Pet. 1:18,19). Why was such an important purchase made? Well, in the analogy of the garment, that you might be "worn," that Christ might come to live inside you, giving life and meaning and purpose to your earthly frame.

In this chapter we will examine ourselves the way a buyer examines a sample garment. First we will see how well we are made and then we will see what purpose we can best serve. In other words, we will progress from our design to our destiny.

First, let's look at our design. The Bible says we are "fearfully and wonderfully made" (Ps. 139:14). We certainly don't have to search far to be convinced of the truth of that statement. Just consider one small part of us, our eyes. They are better than intricately designed cameras. We have an iris and pupil that regulate light, a lens that bends the rays, a retina that registers an upside-down image, and an optic nerve that sends that image to the brain. And presto! We see right side up. Isn't that marvelous?

Furthermore, our eyes are capable of making adjustments instantly. We don't have to turn a knob to get the skin color right or adjust the vertical hold to get the lines out of the picture. The picture is always correct. For example, we can focus on stars trillions of miles away and in the very next instant focus on our finger touching the end of our nose. Amazing! We can snap a picture of the sun with its great intensity of light and immediately snap another of the tiny flicker of a match in a dark room. And both pictures will come out perfectly. We can photograph great vistas of sky, earth, and horizon or the tiny head of a pin; and we can do so without sliding a lens, covering our head with a tarp, or contorting our bodies to get a better angle.

Our depth perception is equally intriguing. I have

stood at the edge of the Grand Canyon and marveled at the river below. It's a sight that usually makes me feel woozy. Yet I have looked at many photographs of the very same scene—without feeling the least bit unsettled. My eye is of superior design.

Think about the eyelids that cover our eyes. While sometimes they act as curtains shutting out light, other times they serve as windshield wipers cleaning the windows of our vision. Notice the little brushes on the end. They catch small particles of dust. Now glance higher to the brows and notice the bigger brushes. They catch bigger particles of dust and stop perspiration from running into our eyes. Every area of need is cared for, isn't it?

See how your eyes are recessed in your skull? Their location serves to protect them. Blows to your head won't necessarily harm your eyes. Such is our wonderful structure.

Our ears are equally well designed. They function like little pianos with different length fibers to pick up sounds. They can register some 1,600 frequencies which, in turn, are sent to the brain. And marvel of marvels, we hear. Over the years we learn to respond to a great variety of sounds. We become alarmed at the clang of a firebell, relax to the harmony of a symphony, and are aroused by the whisper of a loved one's voice.

Our noses are as fascinating as our ears. They help us breathe. Like the eyelids they too have brushes; but this time the brushes are hidden. They catch dust before it reaches our throats and makes us cough in the midst of a sentence. Speakers especially appreciate noses! In addition to breathing, noses enable us to smell. The variety of scents we can distinguish range from the pungent aroma of coffee to the delicate fragrance of a rose to the nauseous odor of a rotting potato.

Our mouths are a favorite part of us. They have lips for

kissing, teeth for chewing, and a tongue for tasting, swallowing, and talking. Our mouths can get us into a great deal of trouble, but we surely wouldn't want to be without them.

Inside our body is a heart, an amazing machine that works constantly, pumping 2,000 gallons of blood a day. If we live an average life span of 70 years, this tireless organ will have pumped 55 million gallons of blood to every cell in our bodies. Connected to our hearts are pipelines, 100,000 miles of them. Called blood vessels, these different-sized pipelines carry oxygen to various parts of our bodies and carry carbon dioxide back out, thereby keeping our blood pure at all times. As the Scripture says, "The life of the flesh is in the blood" (Lev. 17:11).

Our bodies boast several major systems. We have skeletons for structure, muscles for exercise, a nervous system for coordination, a digestive system for breaking down food and eliminating waste, a respiratory system for exhaling and inhaling air, a cardiovascular system for keeping our blood pure, and a reproductive system to insure the survival of our species. And all of these systems interact with each other in a very cooperative way. Truly we can conclude that we are "fearfully and wonderfully made."

Now, how much are we worth? The answer to that question is a paradox. If you were to reduce each one of us to the elements in a test tube we would be worth only about $5.00, maybe slightly more at today's inflationary prices. According to the humorous list of one author, we have enough potassium in us for one weak shot from a toy pistol, enough fat to make seven bars of soap (though some of you can squeeze out a little more than that), enough iron to make a few eight-penny nails, enough sulphur to chase the fleas from a dog, enough lime to whitewash a chicken coop, enough magnesium to treat one case of sour stomach, and enough phosphorous to make 2,200 match heads.

Yet we have stomachs that can consume our entire worth in one meal. Again, some of us can do considerably better than that. In fact, it is estimated that the average American in his lifetime will consume 12 sheep, 16 cattle, 880 chickens, 23 hogs, 35 turkeys, 770 pounds of fish, and 16,100 eggs.

Although we may be worth only $5.00 in a test tube, one scientist estimates that if the power of the atoms in the human body could be harnessed, a human being would bring close to $8.5 billion. Our value is a paradox without equal.

In some cultures human life is worth nothing: babies are tossed to crocodiles in order to appease angry gods; wives are thrown into their deceased husbands' graves (the wives are alive at the time of the interment); the aged are placed on ice floes to freeze to death. That's the way it is in cultures that have not been "enlightened."

Yet "enlightened" cultures have their problems too, only they're more sophisticated in the way they do things and in the reasons they give for doing them. Youth are sent off to war, expected to make a willing sacrifice for the protection of their country. Fetuses are aborted by doctors before they even have a chance to reach a viable size. And deformed infants are sometimes put out of their misery by being smothered, neglected, or starved. That's the way it is in "enlightened" cultures.

Not even the Son of God escaped the low price tag that is sometimes stuck on human life. He was betrayed for a pittance, a mere 30 pieces of silver, the price of a common slave.

Whatever value we might place on life from our limited human perspective, we must realize that from God's perspective the value of human life is inestimable. What makes it so is the presence of a soul, that special, eternal part of every person. When a body dies, the soul lives on. Christ on Calvary saw to it that the soul redeemed would live with Him. But He also paid the price to save the houses for our souls, our bodies. You don't think He would design a body with such intricacies as I have described only to lose it to the oblivion of the grave, do you? No. God wastes nothing in His economy. We will rise from the grave in our bodies—bodies "conformed to His glorious body" (Phil. 3:21). This is the message of the Resurrection.

So much for our design. Now what about our destiny? Here's where the glory of God comes in. "All things were created by Him and for Him" (Col. 1:16), the Bible indicates, starting with the heavens, progressing to the earth, and finally focusing upon individuals on the earth.

Take a moment to think about that great expanse of space which scientists call the universe. Statistics tell us that one billion galaxies have so far been recorded. In our galaxy alone astronomers have calculated there to be 100 billion stars. Around one of these stars revolves our earth, a vividly colored Christmas ball precariously suspended in the blackness of space, positioned not too far from the sun so that we all freeze to death or not too close so that we all burn up. The magnitude of this wonder leads the psalmist to exclaim, "The heavens declare the glory of God; and the firmament sheweth his handiwork" (Ps. 19:1).

The earth itself brings glory to God in the infinite variety and magnificent creativity it manifests. Think about how different the continents are, some fertile, others rocky, some hiding precious minerals, others arid wasteland. Notice how many kinds of trees there are, some rising majestically to the sky, others spreading their branches near the ground. Sniff the flowers with their diversity of scents. Or taste a sampling of vegetables and take note of how varied they are. Listen to the birds as they fill the skies with sound, some seeming to shriek their displeasure with the world, others cooing contentedly in their nests. Amazing!

Then watch the fish cut through the water with their vastly different shapes. You will see fish with lips, fish with whiskers, fish with teeth, and fish with "wings." God's medley spills out onto the plains. See the striped creatures? The spotted ones? The ones with long necks? The ones with manes? Who could dream up such a marvel of created things except the Great Designer Himself?

No matter how varied the objects of God's creation, however, their destinies are always the same: to glorify the One who made them. Most created things seem to carry out that destiny quite effectively simply by existing and letting their design be seen. But God wants more than passive glory. He wants active, voluntary glory. That's where *we* come in. For no object of God's creation can fulfill its destiny to the degree that a redeemed man or woman can. Only we can verbalize His praise. Only we can stand before others and shout from the depths of our souls, "God is great! He loves me so much that He sent His own Son to pay the price for my redemption. In the power of His resurrection He has invaded my life. Now I can live for His glory. How I praise His holy name!"

Thus we conclude that God has designed us for a very specific purpose: not that we might remain on the rack and receive compliments from our admirers but that we might be put to the proper use of actually being "worn" by the One who purchased us. We must remember, however, that our purchaser is quite uncompromising in how He wants us to "fit." Every thread must conform to the living form within. A sleeve too heavily starched will not allow His arm to move through it. A "stiff-necked" collar will not be tolerated. Neither will a confining, cinched-up waistline. No. The Lord wants plenty of breathing room and free-flowing movement within us. He wants every aspect of our being to be yielded to His will.

So let's offer our bodies to our Lord that He might use them for His glory. Let's yield our minds to thinking His thoughts, our eyes to seeing the needs He sees, our ears to hearing the words He speaks, and our voices to uttering the praises of His name. May He have all the freedom He needs to move unreservedly through us.

We are the original creations of God, designed by Him for His special destiny. With a price tag like ours, we can't afford to be smug about our labels. Let's pull them out as often as possible for all the world to see. In that way not only will we feel good about ourselves but also our worthy Creator will receive the credit due Him. His signature will be written on our lives.

Study Questions

1. How much is a human being worth? What makes him so valuable?

2. What responsibility does such a high price tag place on us?

3. How does nature glorify God? What can man do that nature can't in bringing glory to God?

NINE

Discovering My Gifts

The Bible teaches that when a person commits his life to the Lord in a salvation experience, two entirely different transactions take place. First, Christ becomes part of the new believer and, second, the new believer becomes part of Christ. If I am the new believer then Christ has come to indwell me. This is the truth we were reminded of in the chapter we just read. But in an equally real sense, I have also become a part of Christ, for new believers are placed into the church universal, that great living organism which is sometimes referred to as the "Body of Christ."

At the time of his salvation the believer receives a spiritual gift which tells him what part of the Body he is. For example, he may be an eye that sees, an ear that hears, a hand that helps, or a foot that travels. Whatever part he is, his primary responsibility is to help the rest of the organism function properly to the glory of God.

The purpose of this chapter is to help you, the reader, discover what part of the Body you are; in other words, to help you find the niche in God's service where you can be used most effectively to radiate His glory. Discovering your gift will also help you to eliminate areas of service that could prove less than productive.

Before we examine the different parts of the Body, however, we need to recall a few basic truths. The first one is that spiritual gifts and natural talents are not necessarily

the same thing. In the providence of God they may coin-
cide, or in His providence they may not. Your spiritual gift
may lie in the area of your natural strength. Or, as we have
already seen, it could lie in the area of your natural weakness. I mention this phenomenon simply because some
people go through their entire Christian experience
searching but never finding. The reason for their frustration is that they often ruled out the possibility that God
might want to use their weak areas for His glory. In actual-
ity, God delights in using our naturally weak areas. That's
where His supernatural power can positively explode.

Another thing I want to mention is that as Christians all
of us are little "Christ-ones." In other words, in our daily
Christian experience we will all exercise eye gifts, ear gifts,
hand gifts, and feet gifts and actually become quite proficient in the use of some of them. So as we examine the
various body parts you may identify easily with many of
them. Since the purpose of this exercise is to single out
your *special* niche, try to refrain from over-identification.
Instead, pray that God will reveal to you the one area that
He wants to use, not in a natural way but in a *supernatural*
way. Ask Him to show you the gift He has given, not for
your own personal development but for the edification of
the whole Body of Christ. This will be your spiritual gift.

It is possible that as we go through the list of gifts you
may have a reaction exactly opposite to the one mentioned above. Instead of identifying with all the gifts you
may identify with none. This is an equally frustrating position, for the Bible teaches that every Christian has at least
one spiritual gift (see 1 Cor. 12:7). So by the process of
elimination, ask God to show you what your gift is. There
will probably be some gifts that you *know* you do not
possess. Praise the Lord for this discernment. But don't
become over-zealous in your elimination. Eliminate with
the idea of exercising the gift or gifts that remain.

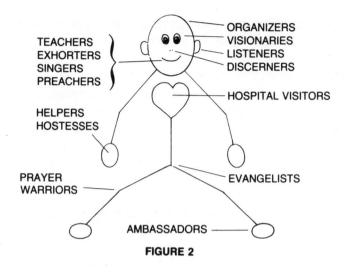

FIGURE 2

Look at Figure 2. If you start at the head of the Body of Christ and proceed to the tip of the toes, you will discover that the spiritual gifts listed in the Bible fall into several major categories. First there are the "brains." These are Christians with gifts of leadership, administration, wisdom, and organization. They love to put programs together and to give orders to other people. If their gifts are developed to the glory of God, church leaders should be able to cause great things to happen for the sake of the kingdom of God without personally receiving any glory whatsoever. Unfortunately such instances are rare.

Next come the "eyes." Christians who have great vision fit into this category. They are able to see beyond present reality into future dreams, to push the church in a direction of progress, to dare to attempt great things for God. To develop properly, these visionaries must run the Christian race with blinders on, for distractions are everywhere including the stumbling runners beside them and the clamorous spectators watching them. A focused vision is essential to those with the "eye" gifts. They are the ones who propel the church forward to bring God glory in ways that the rest of us would never even consider.

There are also "ears." Christians with the ability to listen intently comprise this part of the Body. Because they are able to discern what lies behind the words being spoken to them, they make good counselors. They hear the cry of the heart rather than the cry of the lips. Furthermore, they enjoy becoming involved in the problems of fellow believers. If the ears are to be used for God's glory they need to lock up what they have heard and keep it confidential. There is nothing more grotesque than a mouth in the spot where an ear is supposed to be.

Included in the Christian anatomy are "noses." If you are this part of the Body of Christ, be careful. You can get into a great deal of trouble. The "nose" gift is the gift of discernment. It smells trouble. It intuitively senses who the fakes in the church are and where there is likely to be friction between personalities. The "nose" gift is not a particularly pleasant gift to have but it is a very necessary one. If exercised properly it will enable the church to identify problems *before* they occur rather than painfully dealing with them afterward. Just make sure that if this gift is yours you handle it with God's glory in mind.

There is one more active part of the head, the "mouth." Singers, speakers, exhorters, and preachers make up this portion of the Body of Christ. Their gifts are praising the Lord in song, explaining the Word of God, telling a brother how to "shape-up," and arousing listeners to action. Christians who are "mouths" usually enjoy being in the limelight. For this reason, the "mouth" of the Body of Christ has to be especially alert to the danger of stealing from the Lord His glory.

As we move farther down the Body, we come next to the "heart." This body part is comprised of Christians who genuinely love other people. Their entire manner exudes mercy, compassion, tenderness, and caring. For this reason these folks are excellent at hospital visitation. The person with a "heart" gift sets the beat by which the rest of the Body functions. He is never too busy to "rejoice with those who rejoice" or "to weep with those who weep." He is always ready to greet a newcomer with a smile or to slap an old friend on the back. He gives and gives of himself, never looking for return on his investment. In fact he actually feels most at home when ministering to people in difficulty. Here he can pour out his heart of love and leave a lasting impression for Christ. What a marvelous way to glorify God!

Extending from the "heart" are the "hands." These are Christians who are willing to help anybody do almost anything at any time of the day or night. Ministering physically, these workers attack the most unglamorous jobs in the church. You will usually find them in the nursery, in the kitchen, on the parking lot, or wherever there's a necessary job to be done. And they won't be complaining about their task. God has given them a willingness to do the things that other people shun.

Also included in the "hands" is the beautiful gift of hospitality. Those with this specialty love to open their homes for fellowship in the Lord. Because they are organized ahead of time they manage to serve their refreshments quite easily and enjoy their company at the same time. The greatest threat to their gift being used for God's glory lies in developing a "Martha spirit" of being cumbered with so much serving that the purpose for the evening is missed.

We cannot overlook the reproductive area of the anatomy for this body part includes the evangelists among us. For them, propagating the Christian faith is a major reason for living. They feel very much at ease knocking on doors, circulating tracts in shopping centers, and witnessing to the man in the next seat on an airplane. They sense an urgency to share that eludes most people. Furthermore, they see results of conversion that astound the Christian who doesn't possess their particular gift. The area to watch in their lives, however, is the tendency to become too aggressive and proud. Evangelists must constantly remind themselves that their chief end and purpose is not to convert sinners to Jesus Christ. *Their chief end and purpose is to glorify God.* With this goal in mind they are free to let God change the heart of the uncommitted rather than trying—unsuccessfully—to do it themselves.

Of great importance to the Body of Christ are the "knees." These are Christians who are willing to persevere in prayer. They bombard the throne of grace fervently, effectually, and to the glory of God. Being willing to sacrifice their personal desires so that the one they are praying for might receive God's blessing, they become especially effective intercessors. Long after the Christian world retires for the night and long before it awakens again these prayer warriors are wrestling with a holy God. They are the ones who support the missionaries, encourage the pastors, intercede for the sick, and temper the discerners. Without them the church could not function. They glorify God behind the scenes, quietly but quite effectively.

Last come the "feet." These are Christians who are on the go constantly, ministering in various areas. Their ministries cover everything from house-to-house visitation, to itinerant preaching, to church planting, to cross-cultural missionary work. They are extensions of the local church "in Jerusalem, and in all Judea and Samaria, and to the end of the earth" (Acts 1:8). They glorify God more aggressively than some of the other parts of the Body but certainly no more importantly. All of the body parts are essential.

As you have read these paragraphs I hope you have

been evaluating your own spiritual gifts. As has been pointed out, the Bible teaches that everybody has at least one. Some people have many. But to whom much has been given, much is also required. The most important thing you can do right now is to pin down your various gifts and get busy putting them to work.

How do you start? Well, go through the list of gifts just mentioned and try exercising some of them. You won't know if you have the gift of teaching unless you try to teach. You won't know if your gift is leadership if you never head a committee. You won't know if you have the gift of hospitality if you're afraid to open your home. Or the gift of mercy if you shy away from hospitals. Or the gift of evangelism if you never share the gospel.

When you think you might have discovered your gift ask your spouse or a friend to confirm it. Whenever you see a gift that is obvious in someone else's ministry be sure to point it out to him. Sometimes the hardest gifts of all to identify are the ones you yourself have. Should you discover your gifts easily, however, be quiet until they are confirmed. One source of this confirmation should be your own congregation's recognition that the gifts you are exercising have been given by the Lord. After all, it is quite presumptuous to startle them by boasting, "In the Body of Christ I am the brain."

After your spiritual gift is confirmed, set to work developing it. Accept the opportunities offered you to grow in this direction of your ability. Even take the initiative to create opportunities to serve. For example, if you are a teacher start a Bible study for neighbors or a backyard club for children. If you particularly enjoy evangelism, don't wait for your church to ask you to witness. Go to the shopping mall, the local jail, or the rescue mission and start ministering to souls in need. If you have the gift of mercy visit a nursing home this afternoon. You don't need invitations to exercise some of these gifts. The needs are present and urgent. They are crying for your help right now.

Just as parts of the body that aren't used for a while atrophy and wither, so do spiritual gifts that are not developed. To neglect what God has given you is to bury your talent in the ground. Maybe you think the time isn't right. When you take it upon yourself to determine the right time to get out there and serve the Lord you may discover that the "right time" has long since passed. One of the saddest statements a Christian can make is, "I wish I had become involved earlier."

As you grow older in the Lord your spiritual gifts may change. A once-active evangelist may rest his feet in order to exercise his knees. Or a long-time teacher may stop using his mouth in order to start using his ears. Make sure the change in gifts comes from the Lord and not from your own personal desires. God's timing must be sensed in order for Him to be properly glorified.

So then, once you have identified your spiritual gifts turn them over to the Lord for Him to use. The benefits that come to you personally will be many. First of all you will be settled—settled not only in your faith (for the presence of a spiritual gift can confirm the fact that you belong to the Body of Christ) but also in your Christian service. No longer will you have to search for your special niche in life. You will have found it. But more importantly you will have established your purpose for living. No longer will "glorifying God" be a platitude for you to contemplate, but it will be a real and tangible experience being presently proved in your very own life. You will have discovered at least one way—and a very practical way at that—to fulfill the purpose of your creation.

Study Questions
1. List additional gifts that might be considered brain

gifts; eye gifts; ear gifts; mouth gifts; heart gifts; hand gifts; feet gifts.

    2. For what purpose are spiritual gifts given?

    3. Discuss what will happen to the Body of Christ if certain gifts are either de-emphasized or overemphasized.

TEN

Setting Proper Priorities

Do you think that after our gifts have been identified it is possible for them to be overworked? Consider these Christian dilemmas: Should I go to prayer meeting tonight or stay home to help my son with his term paper? Do you suppose it will be all right if I skip choir practice this week to join my husband for an important business engagement? Is it possible to continue attending my Tuesday morning Bible class and still keep my house in order?

Daily the questions come, forcing us to make decisions dealing directly with priorities in our lives. Sometimes the decisions we make are right and God's confirming peace floods our souls. Other times, though, we do what we think is right only to be plagued with doubts, either from ourselves or from family members more perceptive than we are. How are we supposed to know what we should do and when? Is there any guide to life?

Yes, of course there is. The finest guideline in the world is the timeless Word of God. In it we are challenged to set two different types of priorities: (1) purpose priorities and (2) people priorities. If both of these sets are established properly our lives should go along fairly smoothly. If, on the other hand, we get confused in either area concerning the order of importance we are bound to be plagued with problems.

We will consider our purpose priorities first. If the chief end and purpose of man is to glorify God and enjoy Him forever, then each situation in life must be weighed with this purpose in mind. Most of the time we will probably decide that we should spend Wednesday night in prayer meeting. There may be some instances, however, when we decide—and rightly so—to give up a night of corporate prayer to help our children with their homework. After all, children are special treasures from the Lord and the love, time, and concern we invest in them will reap benefits for eternity.

Along the same line, if we have committed ourselves to sing in the church choir then we should definitely attend the rehearsals. Occasionally, however, especially if hubby makes a special request for us to join him for an important function, it might be more prudent to comply with his request than to attend choir practice. We certainly want to keep peace in the family.

Our third example concerns attending Bible study classes. Again, if we have committed ourselves to this opportunity for spiritual growth we should make a sincere effort to be present at the meetings. If, however, there are unmade beds at home, maybe we should skip the Bible class that day. An untidy housekeeper is not a good testimony to the Lord at a Bible study class or anywhere else.

Each day we make choices like these—choices that reflect our spiritual values. To guide us in making these decisions of purpose *God establishes priorities regarding the people who are important to us.* When there are scores of needs to be met, whose needs are supposed to come first? Is the order we have been taught the correct one? Is it really "Jesus, others, then me"? Or does God have a different set of people priorities, one that is more glorifying to Him and less oppressive to us?

I firmly believe after searching the Scriptures that the "Jesus-others-me" list is backward, specifically in the last two categories. Why, that order puts us on the bottom! Is that where Christians are supposed to be—on the bottom rung of the ladder? Or are we seated in the heavenlies with Christ, emptying ourselves in service from a position of exaltation?

As I understand it, our importance is directly under God's. For only as we cultivate our special relationship to Him will we be able to minister to anyone at all. Therefore I believe the order should read: Jesus, me, then others.

Let me explain this unusual reversal of pronouns. I'll begin with a point of agreement. God must always come first. That fact is indisputable to the Christian who is sincerely seeking to glorify God with his life. Having the Lord at the top of the list means that we won't set out to do our own thing without first subjecting that thing to His approval. But it also means that God will dictate the order in which the rest of the people fall.

By calling us out of the crowd into a personal relationship with Himself, God has said, "You are special to me. Now strengthen our relationship daily that you might become a good minister to others. Draw continually from my well of living water. There you will find the resources you need to keep yourself from running dry. Love, patience and tact will abound as you dip into my spring of refreshment. Therefore guard your trips to the well very jealously."

I personally have taken my Lord's command quite seriously. I schedule my devotional time each day. I find that it must be planned or I have no assurance of getting it. And it must be planned in a way that nobody—and I mean nobody—interferes with it, except in emergencies.

In my early days of motherhood I discovered a great need for discipline in my home, not only in my own life but also in the lives of my children. I required them to take daily afternoon naps. In fact they were expected to continue napping until the day they went off to school. Now I admit I couldn't force my boys to sleep. But I could require them to rest in their rooms for an hour. This I did. As they grew older and realized that they were the only children on the block who weren't allowed to play in the early afternoon, one of them asked me, "Mom, how come I gotta nap?" And I answered, "Your naps are for Mommy, not for you. Mommy needs time to be alone with Jesus." There were many "buts" on his lips, but that was the end of the discussion. I have never regretted that decision.

Every afternoon as I emerge from my sanctuary I am ready to meet the needs of my family. Many times it is not only my family that demands my attention but many other people as well. My appointment with God having been successfully kept, the "others" start taking their proper places in my ministry. I realize, for example, that my husband is more important than my children. I had a marriage before the children entered it and hope to have a marriage after the children leave it. I must admit that there are times when children consume almost *all* of the mother's time, especially during those early years. But a wife must never forget her husband. It is he who has given her the children.

Parental careers come after family involvement and are to be sacrificed to the needs of the family. Sometimes it is wise for a businessman to turn down a job relocation in order to let his children finish school with their friends. Usually it is prudent for the mother to refrain from working while her children are still at home or, if she does work, to make sure she's home by the time school is out. I realize that with divorcees, widows, and families in extreme financial straits, exceptions have to be made. And certainly every family has to make its own career decisions before God, and Him alone. But a principle that will keep you pointed in the right direction is this: never sacrifice your family for your job. If necessary, sacrifice your job for your family. People are more precious in the eyes of God than positions are.

Church organizational activities such as board meetings and committee involvements come after the needs of the family are met. Sometimes offers to "serve the Lord" in the church have to be declined in order to "serve the Lord" at home. No guilt should follow this decision. Often church involvements follow job requirements as well. Sometimes a husband *has* to be away from his family and his church to take a necessary business trip.

Our list of priorities must be flexible. There will be times when, because of the urgency of the moment, the order will be altered. Sick children take precedence over well husbands. A business deadline may take precedence over a night of family volleyball. A searching neighbor may cause the whole family to drop everything in order to present to him God's plan of salvation. None of our "people needs" can be met, however, until our "people priorities" are correctly set. That means God first, me second, and others third.

You might ask, "Has this order ever been tested? Is there anyone who has successfully lived it?" Yes there is. His name is Jesus Christ. Not only did He have His purpose priorities set but He had His people priorities set as well. Notice how carefully He guarded His quiet time with His Father. Wherever the Son of God went He was thronged by multitudes of people, and Jesus, upon seeing them, "was moved with compassion for them, because they were like sheep not having a shepherd. And He began to teach them many things" (Mark 6:34). Sometimes, however, the press of people got so great that "He Himself often withdrew into the wilderness and prayed" (Luke 5:16). Such withdrawal was absolutely necessary to keeping His ministry effective.

Limiting involvement is equally necessary in our own ministries of outreach. It is quite impossible to meet all the needs of all the people in our lives. We have to make repeated selections—selections as to the urgency of the petitions presented, the amount of time available in our schedules, and our suitability to the type of ministry called for. We must guard against spreading ourselves too thin. We want to approach those we are serving with freshness, never frazzled from having to pour out more than we are receiving, never overextending ourselves to the point of ineffectiveness. It is better to minister to a few individuals with our bounty than to a host of people with meager rations. Effective ministry must come from our overflow and not from our reserves.

There will be times in our lives, of course, just as there were times in the life of Christ, when our outreach will extend to great numbers of people. That's good. However, when the pressures of that type of ministry get too great we will feel the need to retreat from the mob. It may be the "mob" we're teaching, the "mob" we're entertaining, or the "mob" we're living with in our house. At any rate, we need to get away for a while.

Any effective outreach requires the balance of solitude. Our refreshing may come from various sources: from an hour alone with the Lord in our bedroom, from a vacation with a loving spouse, or from an evening with a special circle of friends with whom we know we are "safe." Wherever it comes from, however, it is an absolute necessity to a healthy state of mind. We should never feel guilty for desiring it. Someone has aptly said, "If you don't come apart and rest awhile, you will come apart."

So, when the press of people needing attention in your life gets so demanding that you feel like running away, go ahead and run. Get off by yourself and be quiet. Think about the Lord. Think about yourself. Think about life in general. Then when you have pulled yourself together enough to face the multitudes again, come out of your retreat and minister.

You are here to glorify God. Sometimes that purpose is most effectively accomplished by ministering in ways that are contrary to the Christian norm. But you must realize that you are not answering to the Christian norm. You are answering to the King of all creation. Therefore establish for yourself the priorities that He has set. "Understand what the will of the Lord is" (see Eph. 5:17). Once you have done that, "Be filled with the Spirit, speaking to one another in psalms, hymns, and spiritual songs, singing and making melody in your heart to the Lord, giving thanks always for all things to God the Father in the name of our Lord Jesus Christ" (Eph. 5:18-20). Then "Submit yourselves to one another in the fear of God" (see Eph. 5:21). This submission in service will come naturally once the other priorities are established properly. God and His glory, you and me as vehicles of that glory, and others as the beneficiaries. This is God's order; this is God's purpose. It is a very meaningful way to live.

Study Questions

1. Put the following list of responsibilities in the order in which they fall in your life at this particular moment: relatives; job requirements; spouse; God; world needs; friends; church activities; children; neighbors.

2. Now reorganize the list as you feel God wants it to read and if possible support your placement with Scripture.

3. What changes will you have to make in order to achieve this more biblical order?

PART III

An Alertness to Dangers

ELEVEN

Surviving Life's Pressures

Sometimes our priorities are tested by the pressures under which we live. Listen, for example, to the internal voices that demand our immediate attention: Scrub the kitchen floor! If you don't do it today the neighbors will think you live in a pigpen. Put the baby to bed at 2:00! If you neglect his naptime you'll regret it the rest of the evening. Make sure you have dinner on the table by 6:00! If you don't feed your husband on time he'll never make his meeting at 7:00.

But how can we eat at 6:00 when Scott has a baseball game at 5:00? And how can the baby get his nap when Susan has an afternoon music lesson? And how can I get this floor washed and waxed if the phone is jumping off the hook? Such are the pressures a housewife faces.

Businessmen and career women are plagued with similar demands: Fill your quota! Have that letter on my desk in 30 minutes! There's a gentleman outside to see you. He's been waiting more than an hour.

How can I see the gentleman when I have five callers on "hold"? How can I type this letter when I haven't even finished yesterday's correspondence? And as for the quota, forget it! It wasn't realistic anyway.

Even the church adds to the pressures of life: Come help me set up these chairs! Plan to stay after the evening service for a short business meeting. Make sure your lesson outline is written *before* you face your Sunday School class! Would you please make cookies for the luncheon?

Pressures. Pressures. Pressures. How is a Christian supposed to survive? Can he accomplish anything of significance if his schedule is constantly being interrupted? Can he glorify God in chaos? What about yesterday's failures? And tomorrow's impossible demands?

In Psalm 90 God addresses Himself to these questions, reminding us of His sovereignty and reiterating our purpose for living. He begins by describing man's years as being carried away "as with a flood" (v. 5). Now we all understand what a flood is. It is no gentle afternoon drizzle. A flood unleashes torrents of water, bursting dams, tearing out bridges, toppling homes, and sending victims scurrying for safety. That's the way life presses in upon us, and God is telling us that He understands our plight.

He then reminds us that He has existed "from everlasting to everlasting," watching nations rise and fall, seeing individuals come and go. While man is frantically living out his years, often in "labor and sorrow," God is constant, a veritable Rock of Ages, a "dwelling place in all generations." Furthermore, He is in total control of everything that happens on the earth, turning to man at a predetermined hour and calling him home to glory (see v. 3).

Therefore we should go to the Source of our help and ask Him to "teach us to number our days" and "to establish the work of our hands" that His glory might appear in our lives. This admonition, of course, brings us right back to our original question about priorities: What is the chief end and purpose of man? The right answer, you recall, is "to glorify God and enjoy Him forever." That simple statement reduces motivation to a very bare minimum—a bare, *exciting* minimum, that is. Our goal for the day has already been set by God. It is to bring Him glory with our lives. That means He is less concerned with the success of our business than He is with the success of our witness in that business. He is less concerned with whether our family members get to where they're supposed to be on time than He is with the attitude with which they arrive. He is less concerned with the tidiness of our house than He is with the various means we use to guard that tidiness. If tension is the tenor of our household then we are not really glorifying God.

In this area I stand just as guilty as many other housewives stand. It's almost impossible sometimes to keep everything running smoothly. Being a wife, a mother, a daughter, a citizen, a neighbor, a teacher, a cook, a maid, a counselor—all within the course of a day—sometimes gets a little hectic. And often I do what I least want to do. I yell. Loud and clear. I'm so glad God forgives me. My family does too. I explain over and over to my children, "Mommy is growing in grace too. Just as you are. Only slower. Please be patient while I learn. I've got a long way to go to perfection."

When these outbursts occur I know it's time to pull away from my problems and look at life from a bigger perspective than the kitchen sink. I have to realize that my home is not a museum. Instead it should be a special haven of relaxation where my family feels cozy and comfortable. I must realize also that my children's schedules are not nearly as inflexible as they appear to be. Missing an obligation here or there is not nearly as important as missing an opportunity for spiritual growth. My teaching ministry must not consume my personality. A Bible teacher who is frazzled before she ever gets to her classes is not a very good testimony to her students. "I am here to glorify God." Over and over again I remind myself of this truth. The truth sets me free from pressure.

When you stand before God in judgment, what kind of questions do you expect to hear? How many times a year did you wax your kitchen floor? How far did you advance in your business? How many board meetings did you attend in your church? None of these questions will be asked, I believe. Because as meritorious as some of the answers might be, not one is our reason for living. There is only one basic question to which life and eternity address themselves. And that is the same question repeated forever, "How did you glorify God?"

In a life of constant pressure, glorifying God is the only goal that cannot be frustrated by circumstances. You may seek a job promotion and never get it or dream of becoming a famous artist and never see your dreams become reality. You may plan to rear a family and be crushed by medical complications, or you may organize a really full day and not accomplish anything at all on your list. If you cannot attain the goals you have set for yourself, does that mean that your life is a failure?

Absolutely not! The apostle Paul is a good example of a Christian who wrestled with the frustrations of not being able to accomplish all he may have wanted to do, yet he came out victorious. He said, "I don't want to have lived in vain, neither to have labored in vain" (see Phil. 2:16). Therefore he adopted as his daily goal, "For to me, to live is Christ" (Phil. 1:21). In reaching this aim he was successful. Day after day he glorified God. When he came to the end of his life he could triumphantly proclaim, "I have finished the race" (2 Tim. 4:7). We fellow Christians should be able to make the same proclamation for we have an edge on other people. God has revealed to us why we are living and, furthermore, has assured us that every circumstance in life can be used to attain our goal.

Let's put divine wisdom into practice. One way to glorify God is to make a list of daily and weekly activities. This simple task gives structure and direction to an otherwise fragmented series of events. We must remember, however, to keep our schedules flexible. Just when things seem to be going quite smoothly something invariably happens to send our plans awry. That something is called an interruption. It's a telephone ring when we're busy writing a letter. Or the paper boy "collecting" when we're thoroughly lathered in the shower. It's the dog breaking out of his enclosure. Or a friend bursting in with a problem.

Sometimes interruptions are urgent. They're a rush to the hospital in the middle of the night. Or a call to come home for the funeral of a loved one. Or an illness that keeps us away from work. These interruptions can drag on and on for months, bringing disability, sorrow, and pain.

In Christ there is victory over interruptions. For if we really believe that God is in control of all things and is ordering our steps each day, then interruptions are not just accidents. They are planned, divine appointments. So next time the telephone rings, think, "This is my chance to glorify God." Try the same reaction with the person at the door. Even the disability or illness has its opportunities for growth of character and patience.

In fact, the health emergency is one of the greatest opportunities of all to glorify God with our lives. In a life-or-death situation people watch us very closely. How we emerge from our trial is a lasting testimony to our faith. It reveals the shallowness or depth of our relationship to the Lord.

Death, of course, is the ultimate interruption of life. It always seems to come at a very inconvenient time. Do you rebel every time you think of your own death or of a loved one being snatched from your midst? This is a natural reaction, I believe, but it helps to remember that God gives the call to come home. Neither you nor anybody else can stop the receiver from obeying. If you think about it, you really wouldn't want to, would you? Suppose God entrusted to you the right to select the date of death. What age would you choose for yourself? What age for your family and friends? Would 70 years be enough? Or 80? Or 90? Or 100? You might settle on 70 when you're 20. But how are you going to think about that decision when you're 60 or even 69? Don't try to take upon yourself burdens too heavy to bear. God has the keys to life and death. Don't ask Him to lend them to you.

Interrelated with pressures and interruptions are the regrets and fears life brings our way. We spend a great portion of our time either complaining about the past or worrying about the future. "If only" we say with remorse. And "what if" in utter terror. Actually, there are no "if onlys" with God. And there are no "what ifs" either. Things with Him happen exactly according to plan. The sooner we realize that, the better.

Dwelling on the past can ruin the present. You may say: If only I had controlled my tongue, maybe I wouldn't have lost my friend. If only I had witnessed to my sister-in-law, maybe she would have become a Christian before she died. If only we had held family devotions, maybe our son would not have rebelled and left home. If only I had said "I love you," maybe my husband would not have had an affair with another woman. If only I had forbidden my daughter to ride with that teenage dragster, maybe she wouldn't have died in that crash. If only, if only, if only . . . These are words that can stifle your purpose for living.

Face the situation as it is. "If only" does not present options to you. In reality you *did* lose control of your tongue. Now make amends with the ones you offended. And go on living from there.

You did *not* witness to your sister-in-law before she died but she will be held responsible for her own salvation anyway. So learn from your failure and do better next time.

You did *not* conduct family devotions and your child

has now left home. Pray for the future not for the past. You cannot undo your mistakes.

You *did* neglect the love of your husband. Now you face the pain of divorce. God has not left you. He wants you to grow. So set about doing just that.

You *did* let your daughter go on that questionable date; now she is dead. Remember God's sovereignty in calling people home and rest your decision with Him.

I remember counseling a woman who was plagued with guilt concerning her husband's death. Her frustrations came tumbling out: "If only I had been there, maybe it wouldn't have happened. I had gone out for an evening with my friends and when I came home I found him sprawled on the floor. His body was contorted and blue. Oh, God," she agonized, "*if only* I had been there!"

Thinking that she had just come back from her husband's funeral, I asked her how long ago it happened. "Six years ago," she said. "Six years ago this month."

Six years ago? I asked myself in disbelief. Six years ago and she doesn't have victory yet?

Not really wanting to lessen her sorrow (for sorrow is God's emotion that purges) but desperately desiring to have this dear, tormented woman experience God's peace, I tried as gently as possible to share the comfort of God's Word. I explained that the date of man's death is set even before he is born. "His days are determined," the Bible says, "the number of his months are with thee, thou hast appointed his bounds that he cannot pass" (Job 14:15). It wouldn't have mattered whether she had been home or not; her husband had an appointment with God. There are no "if onlys" with God. Men live, die, act, and react exactly according to schedule.

This does not mean that men are puppets or that there are no intermediate means to consider.

On the contrary, men are quite free in their choice of

actions. But these actions, whatever they might turn out to be, fall into God's overall plan. Surgery, drugs, paramedics, and ambulances are all God's divinely decreed means of "extending" man's life to meet God's predetermined deadline. Contrariwise, man's inability to act fast enough, his absence in time of need, his lack of medical knowledge, his fumblings and unwitting mistakes—these too are under God's control. In this last case, what may appear to be a premature death is actually right on time in God's schedule. For it is God's sovereignty that establishes man's freedom.

Are you longing for release from a burden? Is it keeping you from glorifying God today? Do as my counselee did. In a moment of earnest prayer lift the "if onlys" out of your past and place them on your Lord. Remember, His shoulders are much bigger than yours.

The past is not the only aspect of time that torments Christians and others. So does the future. "What if?" we worry and fret. What if it snows tomorrow and I can't keep my appointment for the interview? What if my child flunks math and doesn't graduate with his class? What if my husband gets fired and we lose our home to the bank? What if the stock market crashes? Or the world gets plunged into war? What if, what if, what if? These things may never happen at all. And if they do God is sufficient to deal with them.

Life is filled with all sorts of pressures—pressures from past failures, pressures from present obligations, and pressures from future worries. These pressures can be used in one of two ways. They can be allowed to frustrate and defeat us. Or they can be used as catalysts to promote God's glory. If we shift our concentration from ourselves to the Lord we will not be overwhelmed by life's pressures. We will see that instead of being threats to our well-being, they are actually opportunities to fulfill our obligation to

God. Once we grasp our life's potential we should be able to react to whatever comes our way with a degree of patience and peace, not worrying about what *did* happen or what *might* happen but glorifying God in what *is* happening here and now. This attitude will set us free not only to survive the pressures of life but actually to flourish within them.

Study Questions

1. What is the greatest pressure in your life at the present time?

2. How do you think God wants you to handle this pressure?

3. Are there any "if onlys" in your life? And "what ifs"? Mention them to the Lord in prayer right now.

TWELVE

Making the Most of My Time

One of life's most pertinent pressures is the ever-present, ever-ticking clock. "Hand your paper in on time! Don't be late for your appointment! Get up and get busy; you're wasting precious moments!" Daily the demands harangue us. Time is something we never seem to have enough of. It passes so quickly that it often leaves us wondering where it went. Every once in a while it is wise to remind ourselves of the poem that reads:

> Only one Life
> 'Twill soon be past
> Only what's done
> For Christ will last.

Here we are again, right back to our purpose for living. Since in this chapter we are approaching it from the subject of time, let me ask you a question. In the light of eternity, what have you done with the time that you have been given?

That's a sobering thought, isn't it? Let's examine its ramifications. If measured by the lifetime, some people obviously have much more time to use than others have. If measured segment by segment, however, everybody possesses exactly the same amount. That calculates out to be 24 hours in every day and 60 minutes in every hour. "Why is it, then," you earnestly ask, "that I don't accomplish nearly as much as other people do in the same prescribed period of time?"

Well, for one thing, maybe you're a procrastinator. You put off until tomorrow what you should be doing today. Dwelling on future possibilities is easier than coping with present realities: Tomorrow I'll call Kathy and congratulate her on her husband's promotion. . . . Next week I'll write my parents. . . . In the spring I'll get rid of those dead branches. . . . When I get enough training I want to start a neighborhood Bible study. . . . After the kids leave home I'll be free to do some entertaining. God knows how busy I am right now. And He surely understands. Someday I'll serve Him. Someday . . . Meanwhile, God's clock ticks on.

It is true that in the providence of God some things can be put off until tomorrow. But consider for a moment what would have happened if Christ waited until the twenty-first century to make His visit to earth? What would have happened if He believed that 12 years of age is too young to teach rabbis in the Temple, that a teacher should be at least 40? Or what would have happened if He bypassed the woman at the well because He wasn't yet ready to witness? Our conjectures approach the ridiculous. Why? Because alternatives are nonexistent with our Lord. Christ could not wait until tomorrow to do what had to be done today. He seized each moment for God's glory.

When we study the life of Christ we discover that everything that involved Him occurred at precisely the right instant. We start with His scheduled birth, coming in "the fullness of . . . time" (Gal. 4:4). It was not too early for the gospel to reach every nation and not too late for capital punishment to be carried out by Roman crucifixion, thus fulfilling Old Testament prophecy. But in God's perfect time in a town in Galilee a Hebrew man and woman fell in love. Tracing their lineage back to David, they both anticipated the coming of Messiah. Through them He decided to come. Not a minute too soon, not a minute too late. In fact He was born at the very time Caesar Augustus got the idea that "all the world should be registered"—a decree that put Mary and Joseph in Bethlehem exactly when the baby was due. From then on every event of His life happened right according to schedule.

At the age of 12 Jesus tarried in Jerusalem to make His entrance into the learned sacred world. At 30 He let John the Baptist baptize Him—a sign that His ministry had begun. It was a ministry beset with interference. One after another, people pressed Him to try to get Him to do things sooner than He had originally planned, but He gently set them straight; His mother was the first. At the marriage of Cana she told Him that the hosts were running short of good wine. He turned to her and said, "My hour has not yet come" (John 2:4). When His disciples urged Him to accompany them to the feast of tabernacles He told them to go without Him. His reply was the same as the one He had given His mother: "My time has not yet come" (John 7:6). But He added, "Your time is always ready." Jesus left for the feast shortly after His disciples did but He didn't go with them. Why did He wait so short a time? I believe this situation is recorded in Scripture to show that whereas with us there is a time that is *about* right for action, with Christ there is a time that is *precisely* right for action. Sensing it makes every moment count for God's glory in the fullest possible way.

A word of caution may be in order here. Now is the right time to do something. But now is not necessarily the right time to do everything. God has a schedule for every different activity. The Bible says: "To every thing there is a season, and a time to every purpose under heaven: A time to be born and a time to die; a time to plant, and a time to pluck up that which is planted; a time to kill, and a time to heal; a time to break down, and a time to build up; a time to weep, and a time to laugh; a time to mourn, and a time to dance; a time to cast away stones, and a time to gather stones together; a time to embrace, and a time to refrain from embracing; a time to get, and a time to lose; a time to keep, and a time to cast away; a time to rend, and a time to sew; a time to keep silence, and a time to speak; a time to love, and a time to hate; a time of war, and a time of peace" (Eccles. 3:1-8).

A lifetime of advice lies in these practical words. Our challenge is to discern the appropriate action for the moment, then do what should be done without delay.

Even Christ's death was perfectly timed. When enraged religious leaders of the day "sought to take Him" they found they couldn't touch Him "because His hour had not yet come" (John 7:30). But when Jesus reached the Garden of Gethsemane He sighed at last in submission, "The hour is [finally] come." That hour was not without pain. "Now My soul is troubled," He agonized, "and what shall I say? 'Father, save Me from this hour'? " No. "But for this purpose I came to this hour" (John 12:27).

In seeming victory His enemies took Him then bound Him and spat in His face. In mockery they crowned Him and draped Him in the garments of kings. With scourges they lashed His back then forced Him to carry His cross. In humiliation they crucified Him and left Him to die in His shame. Meanwhile, God's eternal clock ticked on.

Time from earth's perspective took its toll. Throat parched, lungs filled, sinews blazing with fire, the figure hung in pathetic submission. But where the crowd saw only defeat, the heavens saw absolute triumph. For sin after sin was being placed upon the Saviour, and sin after sin was receiving atonement. When at last redemption was accomplished, Christ proclaimed His costly victory to the world. "It is finished," He said. That was all. But it was enough to reverberate to every corner of the globe and to echo its way through the corridors of history. Then quite simply He gave up the ghost, right in the fullness of time.

His friends took Him down from the cross and anointed His body for burial. In a rich man's grave He lay, tightly guarded by soldiers. Time was of utmost importance. "For as Jonah was three days and three nights in the belly of the great fish, so will the Son of Man be three days and three nights in the heart of the earth" (Matt. 12:40). On Sunday morning it happened. He burst from the grave in power. Right on schedule. On time.

It was hard for an everlasting Lord to step into the confines of time. But in order to set us free from its bondage He had to be locked in its chains. For 33 earth-reckoned years He rose every morning and went to bed every night just as you and I do. There, however, the similarity stops. When He came to the end of His days He proclaimed, "I have glorified You on the earth. I have finished the work which You have given Me to do" (John 17:4).

There is only one way that we too can end life with the same proclamation. And that is to seize the opportunity of the moment. You see, God holds both the past and the future securely in His hands. But the time He is primarily interested in is the ever-present NOW.

In eternity where God lives there is no future nor past. There is only NOW. The Bible says, "From everlasting to everlasting, thou art God" (Ps. 90:2; notice the present tense). When Moses asked God to identify Himself to Israel, God replied, "Thus shalt thou say unto the children of Israel, I AM hath sent me unto you" (Exod. 3:14). "Before Abraham was, I AM" (John 8:58). Although these words make the grammarian cringe, they are quite correct theologically. For God is always NOW.

Through the miracle of the new birth this same ever-present God has come to empower our lives. That means that we too can have victory over time. We too can seize the moment and its blessing. But how does it work in practice?

The woman in Proverbs 31 seems to have mastered the art of making the best use of her time. Rising "while it was yet night," she organized the events of her day. She ministered to her family first, "working willingly with her hands." Then she pursued a self-initiated career, "considering a field and buying it" and "making fine linen and selling it." She also had time left over to "stretch out her hand to the poor." One day she received her reward: "Her children rose up and called her blessed; her husband also and he praised her" (see Prov. 31:10-28).

In order to accomplish so much in so very little time, she must have doubled up on her activities. She must have been cooking her dinner while she was sewing a garment and have been teaching her children while she was cleaning her house. What a practical way to "redeem the time."

Today with modern technology on our side we women should be able to accomplish even more than the proverbial "virtuous woman" did, to perform more tasks simultaneously. For instance, we should be able to run a load of clothes through the washer, flip on the microwave oven and heat our dinner, chat with a friend on the phone, and sponge off the gummy kitchen cabinets—all at the same time. And we haven't even touched the spiritual realm. If we really want to make every minute count for God, we can pray while we are ironing, memorize Scripture while we are driving, and listen to the Bible on tape while we are doing almost anything. Such is truly making the most of what could be considered "lost time."

After I learned that there is a spiritual purpose for my life I started feeling guilty about my 20-some pre-Christian years which seemed to me to be a total waste. Upon reaching my thirty-third birthday I was struck afresh with how little for God I had done with the time He had entrusted to me. "Thirty-three years was all the time Christ had," I blurted to my mom, "and look what He accomplished with *His* life."

Tenderly and wisely, Mom turned to me and said, "Peg, Christ had a very concentrated ministry. Most of what we read about Him was accomplished in only three years. The rest of the time was necessary preparation." How true! Christ's ministry *was* a concentrated one. From that point on I determined that I too would have a concentrated ministry, using the preparation God had given me in the past to focus on my purpose for living in the present.

Triumphant Christian living is possible because of our identification with Christ. You see, by His coming to this earth and subjecting Himself to the confines of time, Christ was identifying with our daily defeats and frustrations. But by springing forth from the grave and then coming to live inside us He is allowing us to identify with His victory.

God, therefore, is the One who makes our victory possible. By sovereignly meting out to each of us a certain number of years He is emphasizing His absolute right to every moment of our lives. Whereas the past and the future are important to Him, they are not nearly as important as the present. Did you ever stop to think that every event which has happened to you has been directed by the Lord to bring you to this very moment? Likewise every future action will be a result of how God is sovereignly moving in your life at the present time. So the important question will always be, "How effectively am I letting Him use the time which I have been given today?"

NOW is God's day of salvation. And NOW is His time for service. Every minute the divine clock ticks by has been given not to be wasted but to be invested for eternal returns. With this challenge in mind we should rise each morning and affirm: "This is the day which the Lord hath made" (Ps. 118:24) and then earnestly ask, "How, dear Lord, do you wish to be glorified this day, this moment, in me?"

Study Questions

    1. Finish the statement "Time is . . ."

    2. How did Christ handle the pressure of time?

    3. What do you need to do to make better use of your time? Be specific.

THIRTEEN

Resisting Satan's Distractions

If yielding every moment to Christ brings victory, then the Christian life should be easy. All I have to do is to "let go and let God" and the laurel wreath will be placed upon my head. I can just rest and enjoy God's bounty. Christ will do all the work for me. Right?

Wrong! Absolutely wrong. There is no such thing in Christianity as resting on the laurels of salvation. Our purpose for living must always be guarded, for it can easily be stolen from us. Satan, the one who is usually responsible for the theft, can be a very subtle intruder. He makes a habit of slipping quite unobtrusively into the everyday humdrum of life.

Afraid of being recognized should he enter a situation through the front door, he often sneaks in by the back door, and does so before we even realize there is a stranger present. If by chance we should catch a glimpse of him we might not recognize who he is. For he rarely wears a name tag or flashes a personal identification card. And he frequently appears in disguise, sometimes as a ministering "angel of light" (see 2 Cor. 11:14).

Often Satan masquerades underneath our own selfish desires, tempting us with the philosophy that "since you're a child of the King why don't you see how much you can get out of God?" The suggestion is intriguing, isn't it? On the surface it sounds pretty good. But if we look below the surface we see that the intruder is trying to entangle us again in the same type of servitude from which Christ has delivered us. He is trying to get us back to the place where we are living for self instead of living for the Lord.

The tempter makes suggestions in areas where we are very vulnerable. "Why don't you buy yourself a few more things?" he whispers subtly. "Christians must look successful you know."

Most of us don't need a second nudge to get us on our way to the mall. We buy another car for the driveway, another television set for the bedroom, and yet another suit for the closet. "I must keep up with the Joneses," we rationalize, "especially the Joneses in our church."

Satan is pleased but senses a danger. "Don't become too obvious in your quest for material things," he advises. "Make sure you keep that holy look about you, especially on Sundays when you're taking communion. And just so everybody knows your heart is in the right place, make a pledge to the building fund. Make it large enough to evoke a few 'oohs and aahs.' And make it anonymously—well, almost anonymously. You *do* want to make sure the right people find out about your contribution.

"Good. You're coming along nicely. Now, how about a little relaxation? You've been working overtime in the Lord's service, haven't you? You need to get away for a while. A couple of weeks abroad would do you good. There are some great cathedrals you could see and certainly some missionaries you could visit. We want your trip to be thoroughly 'approved,' you know. Don't forget to take along your most sophisticated camera so that you can document everything on your itinerary. Your slides should make great viewing for the kids back home in the youth group. Just make sure you add some religious commentary to your presentation. You don't want to give the impression that you took the trip entirely for yourself. And, by the way, have a great time. You certainly do deserve it."

Satan's attacks are underhanded, aren't they? They strike with great appeal, even with apparent scriptural support. We all know there is nothing wrong in being the owners of material things or spending money on our own good pleasure. In fact the Lord Himself says that He has given "us richly all things to enjoy" (1 Tim. 6:17). Owning and enjoying are not the problem. The problem arises when "glorifying God" is allowed to become a mere asterisk to our existence instead of our life's very essence and enjoying things takes precedence over enjoying God Himself.

Then we run the risk of experiencing the same frustrations that the author of the book of Ecclesiastes experienced, an author who was, incidentally, a very wealthy man. At his disposal were houses, gardens, pools, treasures, servants, singers, and wine. "Whatsoever mine eyes desired I kept not from them," he boasts (Eccles. 2:10). Yet nothing that he owned really satisfied him.

One day he came to the realization that life is very fleeting. "One generation passeth away, and another generation cometh," he muses (Eccles. 1:4). Yet while people come and go, a cycle of monotony endlessly repeats itself: "The sun also ariseth, and the sun goeth down. . . . The wind goeth toward the south, and turneth about unto the north. . . . From whence the rivers come, thither they return again" (Eccles. 1:5-7). What is the meaning of this change in an unchanging world? Nothing.

To find answers, the writer takes some educational instruction. But this pursuit only increases his questions. More questions add to his misery. "He that increaseth knowledge increaseth sorrow," he says (Eccles. 1:18). People seem to be "always learning [but] never able to come to the knowledge of the truth" (2 Tim. 3:7). The reason for this failure is that Jesus Christ is Truth, and without Him "the wisdom of this world is foolishness" (1 Cor. 3:19).

Yet in our contemporary society the man who wants to get ahead pursues a good education. His education supposedly is the key to a better job. But often the job he ends up taking turns out to be a curse rather than a blessing. He finds that the pressure of business is sapping his strength and ruining his once-perfect health. The drive for advancement is pushing him higher and higher up the corporate ladder of success. But the higher he gets the less secure his position becomes.

From the top of the ladder he looks down and reflects. In the end, was the climb worth it all? His youth is gone. His wife has left him for another man. His children have scattered to the four corners of the globe. And he suddenly realizes that he never even watched them grow up. He feels alone and strangely tormented. Deep down inside he knows that he will soon meet his Maker and be forced to leave his sought-after position to somebody else's management. What a pity!

The writer of Ecclesiastes identifies with this awful feeling of emptiness. He says, "I hated all my labour which I had taken under the sun: because I should leave it unto the man that shall be after me. And who knoweth whether he shall be a wise man or a fool? yet shall he have rule over all my labour. . . . This is also vanity" (Eccles. 2:18,19).

Death seems to add to life's consternation. The possessions a man works all his life to accumulate have to remain behind at his demise. Naked man comes into this world and just as naked he leaves, taking "nothing of his labour, which he may carry away in his hand" (Eccles. 5:15). This period of meditation leads the author to conclude, "There [are] many things that increase vanity" (Eccles. 6:11). In fact, all of life is vanity.

In a sense his conclusion is correct. All of life is indeed vanity, sheer meaninglessness, if the Lord is not in it. When man sees something that he wants he works very hard to get it. Once the prize becomes his possession he has to struggle to keep it. When it breaks, deteriorates, goes out of style, or malfunctions he runs right out to replace it. Meanwhile he is still making payments on his original but worn-out purchase. Things, things, things! They push us, press us, break us, and eventually kill us. Yet to many people, including Christians, worldly things are a measure of success, even a measure of spirituality. "As God's children, you should pursue material wealth," Satan says, trying to sound logical, "then you can tell the world that the Lord's hand of blessing is upon you."

What dangerous thinking this is! Whereas possession of material things may indeed be an indication of God's blessing, it is not always so. In some cases it can be Satan's distraction to keep us from glorifying God. To help us stay on the proper track the Lord asks, "What is a man profited if he gains the whole world, and loses his own soul?" (Matt. 16:26). The Lord puts His emphasis on other kinds of things. "Do not lay up for yourselves treasures on earth, where moth and rust destroy and where thieves break in and steal; but lay up for yourselves treasures in heaven, where neither moth nor rust destroys and where thieves do not break in and steal. For where your treasure is, there your heart will be also" (Matt. 6:19-21). Eternal things have eternal value. In contrast to the deterioration of material things they become increasingly more valuable with the passage of time. So it is important to get your spiritual investment portfolio in order.

Christian families, wake up! It's time for a council meeting. Sit down as a body of believers and talk over the direction your lives are taking. Is everybody in your family dedicated to glorifying God with his life? If not, why not?

Dads, be honest with yourselves. How much is a job promotion worth to you? Is it worth weeks at a time away from your family and a briefcase full of work on weekends? Is it worth yanking your teenagers out of high school, disrupting their education and ending their developing friendships? Is it worth your health? Your marriage? Your purpose for living?

Moms, what about you? Can you handle that job you took to counteract boredom? Are you in control of yourself, your position, and your home? Or are things beginning to press heavily upon you? At the end of the day are your beds still unmade and your breakfast dishes still stacked unwashed in the sink? What about your devotional life? Are you able to fit it in? Or most of the time is your Bible left unopened on the nightstand? And how about your children? Are they participants with you in the exciting arena of life? Or have they been relegated to the stands where the spectators sit, watching their mother exhaust herself as she juggles her various activities?

Kids, you're next. What do you want out of life? Money? Power? Fame? You may work all your lives to get it, whatever it is, only to find that your efforts have backfired. "He that diggeth a pit shall fall into it," the Bible says; "Whoso removeth stones shall be hurt therewith" (Eccles. 10:8,9). Even if you should achieve your goal, you will probably find, like millions of people before you have found, that none of these "things" really satisfy. For "all is vanity" if the Lord is not running your life.

The chief end and purpose of man is to glorify God and enjoy Him forever. This is the only goal in life that is worthy of the Christian's pursuit and the only motivation that will bring him lasting satisfaction. "Delight thyself . . . in the Lord; and He shall give thee the desires of thine heart," the Bible says (Ps. 37:4).

The Christian philosophy of life is not, "OK, Lord, if

you bless me with things, I'll be satisfied." It is "I'll be satisfied, Lord, with you—whether you bless me with things or not." When our lives are based on a commitment such as this, Satan is stopped at the door. He can't sneak past Jesus Christ who is called the "unapproachable light" (1 Tim. 6:16). Confronted by the glorified Lord he will be forced to practice his tactics elsewhere.

But if we hide the Lord's glory in a closet or relegate His radiance to the basement, Satan will be at the door again trying to slither through a crack. Therefore the most basic way to resist being distracted from carrying out God's purpose for our lives is simply to give Christ preeminence in everything we do, to let the glow of His presence do the resisting for us. We who are made for His glory must see to it that we live for His glory. And nothing short of total dedication to that task is acceptable, not to God, not to us, and not to the world that is observing us.

Study Questions

1. What are some of the tactics Satan uses to lure Christians away from their obligations to God?

2. Of these, what do you consider to be the most insidious?

3. Do you agree with the writer of Ecclesiastes when he says, "All is vanity"? What are some of the vain pursuits of your life?

FOURTEEN

Discerning Wolves in Disguise

In the use of diversionary tactics, Satan does not work alone. He has emissaries everywhere, especially in places where we least expect them. Unfortunately, these emissaries have ready prey in us, for we humans are easily diverted. Perhaps that is why the Lord compares us to sheep. "All we like sheep have gone astray," the Bible says; "we have turned every one to his own way" (Isa. 53:6).

The Bible calls Satan's workmen wolves—wolves who, like their leader, are quite adept at disguising themselves. They are especially good at making themselves look like sheep, the very sheep they intend to devour. Such treachery makes them doubly dangerous.

These counterfeit sheep are present within the Body of Christ—present there because anybody who looks like a lamb and talks like a lamb is generally welcomed with open arms. If the new sheep is aggressive by nature he will soon have gathered a following. Just a few nudges here and there and some of the other sheep, who feel the need to be led by somebody—anybody—will have bonded themselves to him for life.

Before long, however, the new sheep will begin to manifest his real nature. This revelation will probably come in one of two ways. The imposter may blatantly fling the Bible down and proclaim, "Listen to me instead!" in which case the more discerning sheep will see their leader for who he really is and flee. Or he may just gradually shift his teaching emphasis to a goal other than God's glory. This goal will not necessarily be evil. It will simply be diversionary. You see, it really does not matter in what direction the imposter leads the sheep. Any direction other than God's direction will accomplish the desired end—spiritual fragmentation. In this latter case, many of the sheep will miss the fact that they are being deceived.

Such tactics pose a real threat to Christians. Is there any way to discern between true and false leaders in the church? For example, let's take a common occurrence. Suppose you, like many others in the contemporary Christian community, are approached with a timely "word of prophecy." How do you know whether the "prophet," who can be either a preacher, teacher, or speaker, is really representing God? How do you know if you should believe what he says? How do you know if you should subject yourself to his teaching? The Lord suggests seven tests.

First, what spirit is dominating the "prophet"? Is it the spirit of Christ or the spirit of antichrist? To find out, give him a verbal test, which he should be willing to take upon your request. The test is so simple that it seems ridiculous. Yet there have been some who have stumbled at it, finding the words impossible to utter. These are the words: "Can you affirm that Jesus Christ is come in the flesh?" (See 1 John 4:3.)

Second, is the "prophet" personally leading a God-glorifying life? The Bible says, "Beware of false prophets, who come to you in sheep's clothing, but inwardly they are ravenous wolves. You will know them by their fruits" (Matt. 7:15,16). In Galatians the Lord contrasts the "works" of the flesh with the "fruit" of the Spirit. Whereas the one is characterized by "adultery, fornication, uncleanness, licentiousness, idolatry, sorcery, hatred, contention, jealousy, outbursts of wrath, selfish ambition, dissensions, heresies, envy, murders, drunkenness, revelry, and the like" (Gal. 5:19-21), the other is characterized by "love, joy, peace, longsuffering, kindness, goodness, faithfulness, gentleness, self-control" (Gal. 5:22,23). What a contrast. Look for evidence of God's presence in any Christian leader's personal life.

Third, is the "prophet" exalting the Lord or is he leading you away from the Lord and His direction for your life? This test, a very crucial one because it brings us back to our purpose for living, is so important that in Old Testament times a death penalty was inflicted on all who could not pass it. The Bible says, "That prophet . . . shall be put to death; because he hath spoken to turn you away from the Lord your God . . . to thrust thee out of the way which the Lord thy God commanded thee to walk in" (Deut. 13:5). Can you imagine what would happen today if the same punishment were still being enforced?

Fourth, if the message being preached involves predicting an event, watch to see if that event comes to pass in every single detail in which it was originally prophesied. Remember God's prophets are not 99.44 percent correct. They are 100 percent correct. A prophet who is correct a majority of the time is still not a prophet of God. The Bible says, "When a prophet speaketh in the name of the Lord, if the thing follow not, nor come to pass, that is the thing which the Lord hath not spoken, but the prophet hath spoken it presumptuously" (Deut. 18:22). This test will necessarily take time, but if there is enough time to make it, it will be very conclusive.

Fifth, does the "prophet" expound the Scriptures, or does he substitute his own words instead? If he quotes messages which sound suspiciously like the King James version of the Bible but can't actually be found within the

Bible, be careful. He is not a prophet of God. About such false teachers the Lord says, "They speak a vision of their own heart, and not out of the mouth of the Lord. . . . I have not sent these prophets, yet they ran: I have not spoken to them, yet they prophesied. . . . Behold, I am against the prophets . . . that use their tongues, and say, He saith" (Jer. 23:16,21,31).

Sixth, do other present-day Christian leaders support the message in question? They should. The Bible says, "The spirits of the prophets are subject to the prophets. For God is not the author of confusion but of peace" (1 Cor. 14:32,33).

Last, does the Bible itself confirm the preacher's message? It must. God says, "In the mouth of two or three witnesses every word shall be established" (2 Cor. 13:1). Certainly the Scripture is the most reliable witness we have. If there is anything at all within it that contradicts what you have been told by the "prophet," dismiss his message immediately. It cannot possibly be from God. The Lord says, "Thou shalt not add [unto the Word which I command you], nor diminish from it" (Deut. 12:32).

The Bible is God's direct communication to man and is man's primary source of guidance and truth. This is not to say that the Lord is limited to speaking through His Word. He can speak any way He wants to. He can speak through visions as He did to Daniel. Or through dreams as He did to Joseph. He can speak through a voice as He did to Moses. Or through the stillness as He did to Elijah. He can speak through counselors to give you advice when you need it. Or through circumstances to funnel the direction of your life. There is one test, however, to which each of these communications must be subjected. That test is the *standard of the Word of God.*

In contrast, the Word of God itself does not need to be tested. It has already passed the scrutiny of the ages. Every single prophecy concerning the birth, the ministry, and the death of our Lord Jesus Christ came to pass in every detail in which it was given. His birthplace was identified 700 years before His birth took place. The prophet Micah foretold, "But thou, Bethlehem Ephratah, though thou be little among the thousands of Judah, yet out of thee shall he come forth unto me that is to be ruler in Israel; whose goings forth have been from of old, from everlasting" (Mic. 5:2). His betrayal, complete with the amount of money paid for the deed, was foretold by the prophet Zechariah. He said, "So they weighed for my price thirty pieces of silver" (Zech. 11:12). His death by crucifixion was prophesied in ghastly detail by His ancestor David: "All my bones are out of joint . . . my tongue cleaveth to my jaws . . . they pierced my hands and my feet . . . they part my garments among them, and cast lots upon my vesture" (Ps. 22:14-18). His resurrection was foretold (see Ps. 16:10) and also His glorious ascension (see Ps. 68:18). Every single one of these prophecies, with their details numbering over 300, came to pass exactly in the way it was prophesied.

Likewise every event concerning the future of the world and the second coming of Messiah as King will also come to pass as foretold. Of the 40-some authors who wrote the Holy Scriptures, not one of them contradicts the prophecy of another. On the contrary, they support each other in the minutest detail. So why fool around with prophets who are questionable? Go directly to God's reliable source of truth. It will manifest its authenticity so beautifully that every attempt to copy it will be shown for what it is—a counterfeit.

When a sheep has been led astray from this time-tested Word of God and finds itself out of the mainstream of truth, how will the Good Shepherd deal with it? What will He do to bring a lamb back to the task of glorifying God with its life? Well, if the errant sheep hasn't wandered too far and still has eye contact with its Shepherd, a nod of the Shepherd's head may be sufficient to indicate, "This is the way, walk ye in it" (Isa. 30:21). In these less difficult cases the Lord promises, "I will instruct thee and teach thee in the way which thou shalt go: I will guide thee with mine eye" (Ps. 32:8).

If the sheep is stubborn, however, the Lord may have to use more severe methods of bringing it back in line. He may deliberately permit it to wander into enemy territory, subjecting itself to the ravages of wolves. When the lamb is desperate, then the Good Shepherd goes to find it, gently picks it up and carries it home. All the way the Shepherd holds it very close to His heart. In this position the lamb can hear every word the Shepherd speaks, even the slightest whisper. It may even be able to pick up the heartbeat of love that faithfully beats within the Shepherd's bosom. That's how close a relationship the disciplined sheep has with the One who has rescued it. In fact, of all the relationships between the Shepherd and His sheep this one may be the most precious. But the closeness comes only *after* the chastening is over, when the will of the sheep has once again been subjected to the will of the Shepherd.

The Shepherd genuinely cares for His flock. If He didn't care He'd let us stray forever. But He does care. He has made us for His glory. And He wants to see that we live for that purpose. So He rescues us—but not before He disciplines us. This discipline hurts. Sometimes the hurt is necessary.

Discipline can, however, be avoided. If the sheep doesn't stray, it won't be chastened. As we move about in the world with its many diversionary voices we need to listen more intently than ever to the voice of our own Good Shepherd. He is the only One we can be sure of, the only One who will never lead us off on some meaningless tangent. The Bible says, "The sheep hear his voice . . . and

... follow him. .... A stranger they will by no means follow, but will flee from him, for they do not know the voice of strangers" (John 10:3-5).

Such discernment, however, comes only when the voice of the Shepherd has become so familiar that it cannot be mistaken for the voice of anybody else, no matter how clever the impersonator may be. If we are truly listening with our hearts to what our Shepherd is saying we will hear not only words of guidance but words of assurance as well. Take, for example, this benedictory prayer: "Now may the God of peace, who brought up our Lord Jesus from the dead, that great Shepherd of the sheep, through the blood of the everlasting covenant, make you complete in every good work to do His will, working in you that which is well-pleasing in His sight, through Jesus Christ, to whom be glory forever and ever" (Heb. 13:20,21).

What a tremendous promise this is! It tells me again that what I cannot do, Jesus Christ can, even in the area of keeping me faithful to my purpose. God *will* be glorified through me, whether that glory comes easily or hard. For He will work "that which is well-pleasing in *His* sight." I need to hear a message like that. Hallelujah!

Study Questions

1. Discuss the seven tests mentioned in this chapter for discerning false prophets. Can you think of others?

2. Of these, how many have you used? When did you use them?

3. Why is the Word of God the ultimate standard for measuring truth and error?

FIFTEEN

Guarding My Testimony

Being distracted from our purpose for living affects not only our personal lives but also the impression we are making on others. Listen to this remark: "If that's what a Christian is, I want no part of his religion!" What a sad, sad statement to hear! It becomes even sadder when you look around and find that the speaker is referring to you.

Tell me, do you think it is a valid remark? Personally, I feel it is. The non-Christian's assessment of believers is, in most cases, painfully accurate. Many Christians don't care what impression they are making on the world. Others care but act oblivious to the fact that God has given instructions for holy living. Even those of us who sincerely desire to live God-glorifying lives find ourselves falling far short of what others expect us to be. If we are honest with ourselves we will probably have to admit that we don't even live up to our own expectations, let alone the expectations of others. What a deplorable state of affairs!

Our lives as Christians should be above reproach. People expect it. And God expects it too. The Bible says, "Walk worthy of the calling with which you were called" (Eph. 4:1). In 1 Thessalonians we are told what that calling is: "Walk worthy of God who calls you into His own kingdom and glory" (1 Thess. 2:12). Ours is a holy calling. And because it is we must be diligent in safeguarding our testimony for the glory of God the Father.

I want to introduce you to a man who forgot the important truth that his calling was to holiness and glory. For the purpose of anonymity we will name our acquaintance Martin. My husband and I met Martin several years ago at a debate on important issues of the Christian faith. As I remember it, Martin was very interested in every subject presented; but when the question of Christian liberty came up for discussion he pelted the debaters with his badly twisted ideas. "Because Christians are assured of their salvation, they can act any way they want to," he argued. Somehow Martin was missing the truth that genuine Christians have been given new natures and *want* to act in ways that bring honor and glory to God.

Martin's loose view of his purpose for living led him quickly into a spiritual decline. After the debate was over he began devoting most of his time to his business. Unfortunately, this devotion occurred at the expense of his family, his church involvement and his spiritual growth. One day he announced that he had purchased some prime mountain property. Keeping an eye on it took him away from home and church every weekend. Then he purchased more property and built several cottages on the whole tract of land. This move kept him from holding any church office because he was never home to attend the planning meetings. Next he built a ski lodge to entice people to buy his cottages. Rationalizing that the public won't invest unless drinks are served he incorporated a bar in his lodge. The next move was predictable. Martin himself began to drink.

On a trip home from his resort one night, Martin suggested to a friend of mine who happened to be accompanying him on this particular excursion that they stop at a bar "for a little pick-up." In the course of a conversation that was getting more and more unrestrained on Martin's part, Martin began mocking "those poor unenlightened

Christians who are bound by their legalism. I'm saved," he continued to philosophize; "it doesn't matter what I do. I'll go to heaven anyway."

In the process of his decline Martin lost many things that should have been dear to him: his family, his church affiliation, and his very closest friends—all because he was selfish in his concept of what Christianity is all about. It *does* matter what you do. The mark of a Christian is a God-oriented life. If a so-called believer is living the same way a non-believer is living he should examine his relationship with God. He may be professing the Lord with his lips but have a heart that is far from holiness. He may never have realized that his chief end and purpose is to glorify God and that God redeemed him primarily for that purpose.

One of Martin's problems was that he was looking at the Christian life from the non-Christian point of view. To the non-Christian a believer is somebody who is shackled by a list of don'ts. This list includes such activities as social drinking, playing cards, going to movies, reading dirty books, wearing makeup, and a host of other things. The non-Christian sees himself as being free to do the things that are forbidden for the Christian. What he doesn't realize is that he, the non-believer, is not free to say no to some of these things. The Christian is free to say no to as many activities as he wishes.

A non-Christian possesses a limited freedom of choice. He can choose only between various means of satisfying his own desires. He is free to do what he *wants* to do, but he is not free to do what he *ought* to do. "For when you were servants of sin," the Bible says, "you were free in regard to righteousness" (Rom. 6:20). The non-believer has no inner ability to glorify God with his life.

In all creation the being with the greatest amount of freedom is the man whom Christ has liberated. "Where the Spirit of the Lord is, there is liberty," the Bible says (2 Cor. 3:17). The Christian possesses the marvelous power to do what he ought to do with his life. He is free to glorify God. And as he sets out to obey his Lord's commands, an amazing transformation takes place. He discovers that what he *ought* to do is rapidly becoming what he *wants* to do. Now he can look Satan directly in the eye and say, "No! I won't yield to your temptation. I am free to reject your control." This is a glorious release from the chains of selfishness and sin.

Once man receives a new nature in Christ he faces some real decisions. He weighs for the first time the question, Do I continue to satisfy my selfish desires or do I choose to magnify my Saviour and Lord? Both are now viable options to him. If he chooses to satisfy himself, his old carnal nature will dominate his behavior. If, on the other hand, he chooses to glorify God, his new nature will grow and triumph in victory. The more he seeks to obey his Lord, the more he will discover that the habits which used to bind him in sin are now being loosed by the power of God.

Therefore true freedom in Christ is really a willing servitude. "Having been set free from sin, you became servants of righteousness," the Bible says (Rom. 6:18). This is the picture of a slave who voluntarily submits his life to a new master and has a hole bored through his ear as a symbol of his vow of obedience. Now his consuming desire is to please the one who has set him free from his previous bondage.

Such a motive implies great responsibility. In order for the Christian to maintain a good testimony to the glory of God he has to weigh his choices carefully. To help us decide what to do in different situations the Bible presents three areas of advice: (1) the area where positive commands are given; (2) the area where negative commands are given; and (3) a gray area where there are no commands at all, only principles to be applied. In other words, there are things to do, things not to do, and things that are open to choice. It is the last area that causes problems.

The first area, the list of positive commands, poses few difficulties for the Christian. Whereas he might choose not to obey all that God requires, he has no problem understanding what is expected of him. God speaks and the Christian listens. For example: "Remember the sabbath day, to keep it holy" (Exod. 20:8); "Pray without ceasing" (1 Thess. 5:17); "In everything give thanks" (1 Thess. 5:18); "Bear one another's burdens" (Gal. 6:2). God is telling us that these are the ways He wants to be glorified through our lives. Divine orders require obedience. God expects it. His child knows he ought to give it. And both parties understand each other fully.

The negative commands of God are even easier for the Christian to understand. "Thou shalt have no other gods before me" (Exod. 20:3); "Thou shalt not make unto thee any graven image" (Exod. 20:4); "Thou shalt not take the name of the Lord thy God in vain" (Exod. 20:7); "Thou shalt not kill" (Exod. 20:13); "Thou shalt not commit adultery" (Exod. 20:14); "Thou shalt not covet" (Exod. 20:17); "Do not quench the Spirit" (1 Thess. 5:19); "Fret not thyself" (Ps. 37:1). This list forbids activities that would keep us from glorifying God. Again there is no gap in communication. God spells out certain dangers to be avoided. And man understands every word He says.

The problems come in the nebulous area of life—an area that has become known as "Christian liberty." Here, instead of saying "Thou shalt" and "Thou shalt not," the Lord gives principles which each individual Christian can apply as his conscience dictates. Naturally the questions which arise are numerous. Can a Christian wear a bikini? Can a Christian use eye shadow? Can a Christian play cards? Our questions fall all over each other in their desire to be expressed and answered. Their answers lie not in what a Christian *can* do (for he *can* do all these things) but in what a Christian *should* do. Herein lies the rub.

When faced with a problem on which God is silent, a believer should ask himself four basic questions. These questions are easy to remember because their different directions form a cross (figure 3).

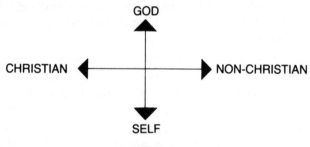

GOD

CHRISTIAN ◄———————► NON-CHRISTIAN

SELF

FIGURE 3

Interrogate yourself in the following way: First, *will my participating in the activity in question bring glory to the Lord?* The Bible says, "Whether you eat or drink, or whatever you do, do all to the glory of God" (1 Cor. 10:31). Since glorifying God is our fundamental reason for living, that is the fundamental question we must always ask ourselves. If the answer is no there may be no need to go further in the questioning process.

If, however, we receive a positive answer or even a neutral answer to the first question, then the second question should be: *Will participating in the activity edify me to the point where I will become a better person?* The apostle Paul warns, "All things are lawful for me, but all things are not helpful; all things are lawful for me, but all things do not edify" (1 Cor. 10:23).

Have you been stopped by any red lights so far? If not, then proceed to the third question: *Will the report that I have taken part in something questionable hurt the testimony I have been trying to maintain before my brothers and sisters in Christ?* Paul took this question so seriously that he came to the following conclusion: "If food makes my brother stumble, I will eat no meat while the world stands, lest I make my brother stumble" (1 Cor. 8:13). How sensitive Paul was to what others were thinking about him!

The last question involves our relationship to non-Christians: *Will my involvement in the activity hinder my testimony to those I am trying to reach with the gospel?* Or, conversely, will it help it? Again the apostle Paul offers advice: "Give no offense," he says. Then he adds his motive: "not seeking my own profit, but the profit of many, that they may be saved" (1 Cor. 10:32,33).

These are our areas of concern. In each area the decision we make will send ripples in several different directions: upward to God, inward to us, and outward to others, believers and non-believers alike. The Bible says, "None of us lives to himself" (Rom. 14:7). How true that statement is! And what a big responsibility it places on our shoulders!

Now suppose two of us are faced with the same decision concerning our Christian liberty and one of us decides to participate in the questionable activity and the other does not. As sensitive Christians earnestly seeking God's will for our lives, each of us has asked himself the four suggested questions and each of us has come up with courses of action that are diametrically opposed to each other. What then?

The Bible says, "Let each be fully convinced in his own mind" (Rom. 14:5). If you have answered the questions honestly and your conscience is clear, go ahead and enjoy a hearty involvement in the activity. The Bible says, "Happy is he who does not condemn himself in what he approves" (Rom. 14:22). If, on the other hand, you feel that you personally cannot participate, but another Christian brother feels he can, remember not to judge that brother. He is exercising *his* Christian liberty just as you are exercising yours.

If, however, you feel uneasy, perhaps the Holy Spirit is speaking to you. If "to do or not to do" is your dilemma, "not to do" is probably your answer. When in doubt, heed a simple principle contained in the Word of God: "Abstain from every form of evil" (1 Thess. 5:22). A moment of self-indulgence is not worth the price of a broken testimony.

We Christians are called to holy living. But the call does not come without the means for accomplishing it. Along with the power of His Spirit within us, God has given us His Word. In its pages we will find all the principles we need for maintaining a vibrant testimony. But unless we are obedient to put those principles into practice we could find ourselves in Martin's shoes.

"If that's what a Christian is, I want no part of his religion." This is a statement that should never be uttered. Wouldn't it be thrilling if in its place we would hear over and over again, "If that's what a Christian is, I want his Lord as my Lord too." To this end we have been created and redeemed. To this end we should be living as believers, for it is an end which brings glory to God.

Study Questions

1. Who has more freedom: the Christian or the non-Christian? Why?

2. To whom is the Christian responsible for his actions?

3. Since becoming a Christian, have you noticed a change in your actions? How about in your desires? Elaborate.

PART IV

An Effective Outreach Toward Others

SIXTEEN

Building a Stable Pyramid

If we have a right orientation toward God, a proper attitude toward ourselves, and an alertness to the dangers that would divert us from the task of glorifying God with our lives we should be ready to be used to reach others with the same enlightenment that we have received. Now how do we go about doing it?

Let me illustrate with an analogy that I am borrowing from archaeology. Consider the pyramids of Egypt. What marvelous feats of engineering they are, especially when you realize that they were constructed thousands of years ago, long before modern technology had been developed. We marvel at how the workmen performed their various tasks so accurately without the aid of precision instruments. We don't know everything they did. But one thing we do know. They built from the bottom up. They started with a solid base and then added progressively smaller layers of stone until they came to the finishing touch: the apex. They followed the architect's blueprint so closely that the completed work is within an inch or two of perfection. The result is that today, centuries later, the Egyptian pyramids are still standing, just as awesome as ever.

What do you think would have happened if the Egyptians had built their pyramids upside down—if they had formed the apex first, jammed its peak into the ground, then started adding layer after layer until they finally came to the massive foundational stone? Why, that's ridiculous, you say. Their structure would have crumbled in the beginning stages of the building process. True. And those of us living today would be deprived of the awesome experience of witnessing their beauty. Perhaps we would not even be aware that such things as pyramids existed at all.

At this point, Christian, I want to speak very directly. You may be quick to agree with the necessity of building any structure properly. Yet when it comes to building a pyramid of priorities for witnessing for your faith are you making the same mistake you consider ludicrous in our analogy? Are you starting your pyramid at the wrong end? Are you beginning with the peak and hoping to finish with the foundation? Are you trying to win souls through manipulation and coercion, then hoping that the end will somehow glorify God? God is not glorified through human efforts to please Him. He is glorified through vessels yielded to His leading who are willing to follow His blueprint.

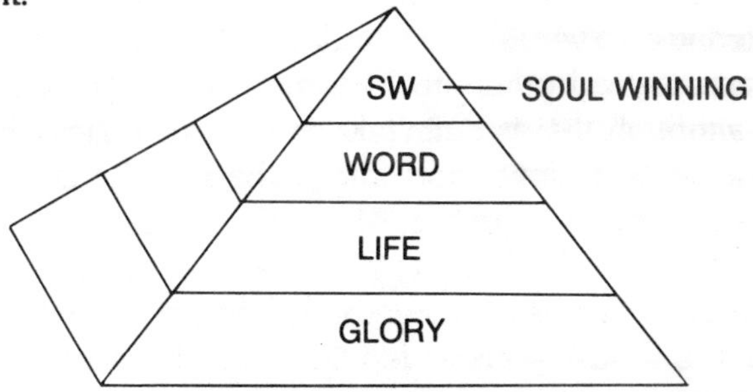

FIGURE 4

You will see in figure 4 that the foundational stone for effective Christian outreach is not soul winning. It is a sincere desire to glorify God. Once that basic motive for living has been established it should be covered with a life dedicated to holiness. People usually want to see Christ in our lives before they are willing to accept His Word from our lips. Yet how many activists are running around presenting the gospel with no conception at all of what it means to live a life that is beyond reproach in the eyes of a world that is watching every move! How many Christians are ready to spout forth carefully memorized salvation verses without first preparing the hearer for the Word's reception by showing him love? I myself am learning these truths through my own personal failures. I am discovering that it is my life that paves the way for God's Word just as it is God's Word that paves the way for soul winning. These four levels of priorities, laid in the proper order, will construct a lasting memorial to God. After all, He is the Architect who drew the plans for effective Christian witnessing in the first place and then passed them on to us so that men all over the world might enjoy the results of His wisdom.

Soul winning, important as it is, should not be the exclusive goal for any Christian's life. If it is, that Christian should take a second look at his pyramid of priorities, for it is teetering on a very shaky foundation. God did not create mankind to lead others to a saving knowledge of Himself—although that is definitely *part* of our obligation as children of God. Nor is God going to base His judgment of our lives on the number of souls we bring into the kingdom.

Can you imagine how embarrassed you would feel if the Lord turned to you on judgment day and asked, "How many scalps have you got on your belt?" Of course I don't imagine He would express Himself exactly that way. But regardless of how it was put, the average Christian would respond by shrinking in silent humiliation while the proud soul winners would puff out their chests and recite their recorded triumphs.

God will not put us through such judgment because

God did not create us to compete with others for numbers. He made us to glorify Himself. "You were bought at a price," the Bible says; "therefore glorify God in your body and in your spirit, which are God's" (1 Cor. 6:20). This is a very broad purpose. It has to be. It must include every human being who has ever been born and, furthermore, include him in whatever circumstances he might happen to find himself. It must apply to people with no means of outreach whatsoever, or very limited outreach at best, such as lonely explorers shivering in the Arctic, frustrated invalids on beds of affliction, or victims of limiting physical handicaps. While such individuals may not have the opportunity of introducing someone to Christ, each one can lead a successful Christian life. For success is not measured by the number of conversions. Success is measured by how we bring glory to the King of kings and Lord of lords.

Life's ultimate goal of glorifying God can be reached in various ways: by dwelling on thoughts that are holy and pure, or by manifesting a "gentle and quiet spirit, which is very precious in the sight of God" (1 Pet. 3:4); by exercising the gift of hospitality, or by rendering a talent to the Lord; by choosing to speak a word in love, or by quietly weeping with someone who hurts; by rejoicing with a brother who is happy and successful, or by helping a fallen one to rise to his feet; by giving a cup of cold water to the thirsty, or by feeding the starving and clothing the naked; by exalting the Lord with a song or a testimony, or by leading lost sheep home to the fold.

Soul winning is one way—one way among many—to glorify God with a life sold out to Him. To make it the all-important goal for living, however, is to bring upon yourself unnecessary guilt and frustration. For how many souls are enough to please a demanding God? What if you don't win even one? Then truly, according to your own assessment of your life, you will have run the race in vain. If on the other hand you forget numbers and embrace the God-given goal of glorifying Him you will be able to stand before Him in judgment and say with the apostle Paul, "I have finished the race, I have kept the faith. Finally, there is laid up for me the crown of righteousness" (2 Tim. 4:7,8).

If any of you really want to become soul winners, the Bible has some advice for you. Stop praying so much for the people you want to reach and start praying more for yourself. After all, you are the vessel God is going to use. An appropriate prayer to offer is Psalm 51. Penned by David after his sin with Bathsheba it acts as a spiritual pipe cleaner. Its strong emphasis on confession is sure to scrape out any personal sin that might be a hindrance to your daily witness. Just think how purged you would be if you began every day with these words: "Have mercy upon me, O God . . . blot out my transgressions. Wash me thoroughly from mine iniquity, and cleanse me from my sin. . . . Purge me with hyssop, and I shall be clean: wash me, and I shall be whiter than snow. . . . Hide thy face from my sins, and blot out all mine iniquities. Create in me a clean heart, O God; and renew a right spirit within me" (Ps. 51:1-10). After verse 12 the psalm makes an abrupt break. The next verse promises that the cleansed life will be used by God as a soul winner—almost automatically. Look at what the psalmist says: "Then will I teach transgressors thy ways; and sinners shall be converted unto thee" (Ps. 51:13).

Isn't that exciting? God's formula for effective witnessing is to move up the pyramid as He directs, reflecting His glory through your life and then letting Him use that life as He sees fit.

After your life is cleansed by confession, take heed how you speak, "For out of the abundance of the heart the mouth speaks" (Matt. 12:34), the Bible says. Every word should be filtered for sensitivity to the needs of the listener, whether it is a word of yours or the Word of God. Remember that few souls, if any, are won through arguments. Rather, souls are won through the penetrating Scriptures. The Bible states very simply how faith comes: "Faith comes by hearing, and hearing by the word of God" (Rom. 10:17). Even the Word of God, however, needs to be handled delicately.

If you have trouble, as I do, taking the initiative in sharing the gospel with someone, finish reading Psalm 51. It contains a practical prayer for reticent witnesses. It says, "O Lord, open thou my lips: and my mouth shall shew forth thy praise" (v. 15). So the first thing I do is ask the Lord to open my physically closed mouth. Isn't it interesting to notice that most of us can talk on almost any subject quite easily, even with a complete stranger, but the subject of salvation requires us to pray, "Open thou my mouth"?

Anyway, I'm glad the prayer is there because I've had to use it frequently. After I've prayed for an open mouth I ask for the right words. Then I add one more thing: "Please, Lord, trap me into witnessing today." I know my own heart. If I can wiggle out of a witness I will usually wiggle out. But when He traps me I can't get out. That's when sharing my faith starts to be fun.

When God does trap me into witnessing for Him I try to select my words as delicately as possible. The Bible advises me well: "Continue in prayer . . . that God would open . . . a door for the word. . . . Let your speech always be with grace, seasoned with salt, that you may know how you ought to answer each one" (Col. 4:2-6). Every person has a need, but every person's need is not to have God's total plan of salvation dumped on him. Too much salt makes the diner gag. Just the right amount, however, causes a thirst for water. That's the secret for a God-glorifying witness: putting in the right amount of salt—not so little that there's no response at all or not so much that there's a premature death from the overdose, but precisely the right amount. We want to create a thirst for the living water of God.

After the conversation progresses a little we should try to insert some Scripture. This is the seed that is going to produce new life. Remember, the purpose of our words is to pave the way for God's Word. But we should not be discouraged if we get a negative response at this point. For some seed will be snatched by Satan before it even reaches the soil of the unconverted heart (see Mark 4:15). Other seed will spring up only to be withered by the sun of persecution and affliction (see Mark 4:17). Still other seed will get choked by the cares of the world, the deceitfulness of riches, and the lust for things (see Mark 4:19). But, happily, some seed will take root and bear fruit. In order to have even a few plants in the last category it is necessary to sow a tremendous amount of seed. For the amount reaped will be in direct proportion to the amount sown. The Bible says, "He who sows sparingly will also reap sparingly, and he who sows bountifully will also reap bountifully" (2 Cor. 9:6).

Once we have done a faithful job of sowing God's Word we can rest the results in His sovereignty. It is the Lord who causes the seed to take root in plowed, fertile soil. As we have seen, the whole process of salvation is of Him. He convicts (see John 16:8), He calls (see John 10:3), He draws (see John 6:44), and He saves (see John 10:28). We can live the Christian life before others and earnestly persuade them to embrace it. But when it comes to the actual act of leading sinners into the kingdom of heaven God brooks no rivals for the honor. He performs the act of soul winning quite effectively all by Himself.

This is not to say that Christians are never active in the

apex of the pyramid, that top part which we have entitled "soul winning." They are. They are the means God uses most frequently to draw men and women to Himself. But they are only means, secondary causes, of salvation. The primary cause is God.

A properly constructed pyramid is not meant to glorify the workers who built it, although if the workers do their respective jobs well they will receive the credit due them. Rather, a finished pyramid brings the most glory to the architect who came up with its design and then saw to it that that design became reality. So it is with the pyramid of life. If put together according to the blueprint, with its foundation laid first, its intermediate layers added proportionately, and its crowning peak placed on top, it will point all eyes to the heavens. From whatever angle the structure is viewed its message should be the same: here is a life that is yielded to God and is letting His glory shine through.

Study Questions

1. Why is the chief end and purpose of man not soul winning?

2. In what ways does the emphasis on God's glory rather than on producing "decisions" free us to be better witnesses?

3. Can you think of some Scripture verses to support the premise that cleansed lives pave the way for the presentation of the Word of God?

SEVENTEEN

Witnessing Naturally

When I was a new Christian I approached the task of witnessing with real evangelistic fervor, not because being aggressive was natural for me (it was extremely *un*natural) but because I felt that it was up to me to bring souls into God's kingdom. Unfortunately, that approach turned more people off than on and I lost many opportunities to witness to them again in the future. I realize now what my problem was. I thought that the number of converts I brought into the kingdom was more important than how I won them. In other words, obtaining results to please God had taken priority over actually glorifying God. Perhaps you are making the same mistake.

Let me ask you some questions. How do you view the challenge of witnessing? How successful have you been in your endeavors? By "successful" I do not mean how many converts do you have to your credit. I mean how effectively have you seized the opportunities that God has brought your way? Perhaps you have tried to imitate somebody else's techniques of winning souls and those techniques have not worked well for you. You wonder why. The reason is that the way God is using the one you admire is not necessarily the way He wants to use you. He wants to use you through your own personality—the one He has given you for that purpose.

Maybe you have taken courses in witnessing and felt very ill-at-ease during the training, as if you were being forced into a mold in which your personality could not conform. I identify with your frustration. I remember attending one course on witnessing that was so contrived that I had to leave the room for fear of getting sick. I thought to myself, *I can't do what those people are teaching. I'm not even sure it's scriptural.* So I chalked myself up as an evangelistic failure and withdrew into my shell.

Then one day while studying God's Word I came upon a series of truths that set me free from the guilt of my failure. I discovered that there are principles of salvation and witnessing which, if applied to one's own personality, will set the Christian free to be a natural witness for his Lord. You see, when God regenerates us He gives us new natures, not new personalities. We may still be as quiet and withdrawn as we were before we became Christians, but now we have God's power putting that old personality to work. That means He can use *any* of us to further His kingdom on earth in whatever way *He* chooses.

The first principle that released me from my hang-ups was the realization that God is the One who saves souls. This principle is so obvious that it seems ridiculous to mention it. Indeed, it would be ridiculous except for one fact: most of us act as if the salvation of the lost is within our own power instead of within God's. We fail to see that unless the Lord opens the heart of the sinner, that sinner will never exercise saving faith. Though God may choose to use men as His instruments, the salvation process itself is all of God, a cooperative work of the Trinity. A Scotchman puts it this way:

> The Father thought it
> The Son bought it
> The Spirit wrought it
> But I've got it.

Not one of us would be able to say, "I've got it" if the Spirit hadn't first wrought it and the Son hadn't bought it and the Father hadn't thought it. So relax. Salvation is God's doing. It was so in your own conversion experience and it will be so in the experience of anyone you may try to win to the Lord.

The second freeing principle of salvation is that God uses a variety of people and circumstances to bring any one person to a point of spiritual commitment. In fact so many people are involved in the conversion of one soul that it is impossible to number them. Take, for example, your own salvation. How many Christians lived godly lives in front of you before you decided you wanted that kind of life for yourself? How many people shared their faith with you before you exercised faith of your own? How many prayers for your salvation bombarded the throne of grace before you yourself prayed the sinner's prayer of confession? How many angels protected you before you came to the point of conviction? How many messages did you hear before one pierced your heart? Where you and I are at a loss to answer, the Bible puts the answer in our mouths: "I know not the numbers thereof" (Ps. 71:15). In all of these situations God was drawing you to Himself long before you ever responded.

In my own life there were many Christian influences. There were several gospel-preaching ministers, a few dedicated Sunday School teachers, a couple of on-fire youth leaders, some acquaintances who lived for Christ in a godly way, and a mother who prayed 20 years for my salvation.

Then one day a man named John Palmer rang my doorbell and invited me to a neighborhood Bible study. Through that study I became a child of God. John Palmer spent exactly nine months with me, teaching me truths from the Scriptures. My mother spent almost 20 years praying for my conversion. My mother did not, as the saying goes, "lead me to the Lord." Yet I wonder who will receive the reward for my soul. Will it be John Palmer? Or my mother? Or both? Perhaps if there hadn't been a mother praying for me for 20 years, there wouldn't have been any John Palmer.

Therefore, Moms, don't stop interceding for your children. Prayer is a necessary part of the long process of God's preparation of the heart. In fact, God uses so many men in so many ways to lead one sinner to Himself that it is impossible many times to tell who deserves the title of "soul winner."

God's process of preparation resembles an automobile assembly line staffed with many workers. One person builds the chassis. Another puts the wheels in place. Still another does the wiring. Yet another adds the upholstery. There is only one person, however, who turns the key and drives the completed car off the line. That Person is God. Sometimes He works alone, and sometimes He works through people. But the last person on the line—whoever he is—cannot do his job at all if the other workers are not faithful to perform their functions first.

You might ask the question, "Who is the actual builder of the car?" The answer is, "All who worked on the assembly line." Another question might be, "Who will get paid for building the car?" The answer is the same: "All who worked on the assembly line." The Bible says, "We are God's fellow workers" (1 Cor. 3:9). And "each one will receive his own reward according to his own labor" (1 Cor. 3:8), so that "he who sows and he who reaps may rejoice together" (John 4:36). In other words, rewards come for *faithfulness* in witnessing, not for results. There are many workers who never get to see the finished product. That, however, does not mean that the product will not be finished. If we come to the end of our lives never having led one soul into the kingdom of God we should feel no guilt whatsoever. We may have prepared many souls for someone else's witness. In heaven we will learn how many.

Often in the process of witnessing, certain people, usually those with the gift of evangelism, find themselves frequently at the end of God's assembly line. Therefore they reap many souls with whom they may not even be acquainted. Such is the case with me. Because I am a public speaker I am often the one God uses to "turn the key" in women's lives. Yet every time I see women respond to the gospel invitation I stand in amazement. I wonder, Who had the foresight to invite these needy gals to the meeting? Who was praying for them while I was speaking? How many people witnessed to them before this day of conviction? Who, out of all the Christians involved, will receive the reward for soul winning? Me? I don't even know the gals. They have heard me speak for 30 minutes and have made a profession of faith. God constantly reminds me, "I sent you to reap that for which you have not labored; other men have labored, and you have entered into their labors" (John 4:38). I pray that I may never forget this humbling truth. *Many* people are involved in one soul's conversion.

It is important to remember that God, not man, is running the assembly line. He is controlling the speed of the line and the placement of people along that line. He is also controlling which car is being put together at any one time. If when a non-Christian (the car) passes by a Christian (the worker) and the Christian fails to do his job, the next person on the line has to do double duty. If, on the other hand, the Christian gets over-zealous and tries to add *all* the parts to the car at once, terrible confusion results in the non-Christian's life. The jumbled parts will probably have to be removed one by one and the car sent through the line again.

The best way to be used effectively on God's assembly line is to remember that your first priority is to glorify God in all things. Then do as God directs. Don't renege on an obvious responsibility. But, on the other hand, don't steal a blessing from someone who is stationed farther down the line. The thing you want to avoid is becoming involved in a contrived, manipulative witness. Instead be sensitive to God's leading each moment. Then you will be a channel for God to move through rather than a force exerting itself to move men for God. In addition you will be freed from any burden of guilt you may have been carrying—guilt for not having produced enough converts to fill your preconceived idea of God's quota.

Although salvation is all of God, God usually accomplishes it through people. Furthermore He accomplishes it differently in every single case through the unique personalities He has given each of us. If we simply yield ourselves to Him each day to be used as He sees fit we will find ourselves gloriously released to be natural witnesses. No longer will we be trying to do God's complicated work of saving souls. Instead we will be relaxing in His sovereignty, ready to be used when called upon.

Readiness for use involves alertness to opportunities. I am convinced that opportunities for effective witnessing are all around us; but for one reason or another we are missing them. The Bible says, "Be ready to give a defense to everyone who asks you a reason for the hope that is in you, with meekness and fear" (1 Pet. 3:15). "Being ready" means praying that God will use you and then watching for the ways in which God is answering that prayer. I like the words "meekness and fear" because that's how I feel when I am witnessing—meek and afraid. That verse, however, is proof enough for me that God can use "fraidy cats" as well as outgoing people on His magnificent assembly line. Perhaps He may even be able to use "fraidy cats" more effectively because timidity makes one extremely sensitive to the possibilities of making a mistake. Timid people want to add precisely the right part at precisely the right time and seem willing to leave the results to God.

I am so thankful for these liberating concepts of witnessing that I want to shout God's praises from the mountaintops. They have freed me from the tension of trying to imitate other people. They have also freed me from the burden of trying to produce results. When I was under the impression that I was the one who was supposed to do the soul winning I would get so uptight about my failures that I would botch up the opportunities God gave me. Now that I am learning to leave God's business to Him, I actually have fun wondering how God is going to use me each day.

Once you've been released to witness according to your own personality life becomes exciting. You can pull yourself away from the situations in which you are involved and watch God work them out. You are free to let Him teach you more effective methods of sharing your faith and free to let Him use other Christians besides yourself to bring someone you are concerned about into the believing Body of Christ. But even more important than that you are free to bring God glory in the way He specifies each day by simply being natural and letting His radiance show.

Study Questions

1. Define a "successful" witness.

2. List the people who contributed to your salvation. Which one was the most influential?

3. What are the responsibilities of the workers on God's assembly line?

EIGHTEEN
Following Christ's Example

One day when I was feeling particularly ill-at-ease with one of the modern witnessing programs that was trying to force me into its mold I decided to search through the Gospels to see what methods the Son of God used to share *His* faith with others. What I found confirmed my belief that there is simply no one "correct" way to witness. Once your motive is to *glorify God* rather than to mass-produce "decisions" you are free to be selective in your ministry and creative in your approach to each individual. You are also free to rest the results of your witness in the will of a sovereign God. In all these areas Jesus Christ is a perfect example to follow. Together let's examine His outreach.

Because Christ's motive for living was to glorify God He was free from the pressure to keep a tally of numbers. If He had been judged on the number of conversions He effected, our Lord, by modern standards, would probably be considered a failure. When He preached His heart out to the masses there were no thousands walking aisles and signing decision cards. In fact many hearers went away completely unconvinced of the urgency of the message they had just heard. Not even all of Christ's inner circle of disciples submitted to His life-changing power. Yet in spite of these disheartening results our Lord had peace. Discovering this truth really blessed me.

Another aspect of Christ's ministry that blessed me was the selectiveness of His relationships with people. Look at the narrowing cone of His involvement as pictured in figure 5:

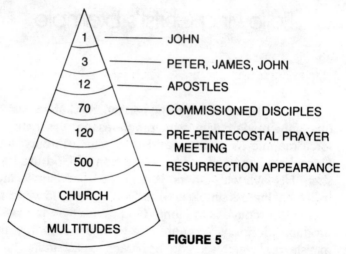

1	JOHN
3	PETER, JAMES, JOHN
12	APOSTLES
70	COMMISSIONED DISCIPLES
120	PRE-PENTECOSTAL PRAYER MEETING
500	RESURRECTION APPEARANCE
CHURCH	
MULTITUDES	

FIGURE 5

Multitudes followed the Saviour. At times He ministered to all of them. From these multitudes Christ chose a church. Every member of the body of believers received and still receives the special ministry of Christ's Holy Spirit. Nonbelievers, however, are not included in Christ's ministry to the church.

After Christ was raised from the dead only a portion of the church was allowed to see His resurrected body, the greatest number being "over five hundred brethren at once" (1 Cor. 15:6). Just before the thrill of Pentecost there weren't even five hundred believers gathered to pray. There were only "about a hundred and twenty" followers present (Acts 1:15). The disciples who were sent out to preach the gospel totaled a mere 70 (see Luke 10:1). These were instructed by the Lord Himself, but not nearly as intensely as He taught His chosen apostles. The apostles in turn comprised a manageable dozen (see Mark 3:14).

Christ's selective ministry did not end with His choice of the apostles. Of the Twelve He chose three with whom to have a special relationship: Peter, James, and John. Yet even from these three He made a further selection—John, the beloved disciple. I suspect that the Lord's ability to stay on top of every counseling situation was directly related to His careful construction of this cone of ministerial involvement.

Several people besides the apostle John are mentioned in the Scriptures as receiving Christ's concentrated attention. As we examine His witness with two of them, notice how sensitively, creatively, and differently the Lord met their personal needs. Take, for instance, the woman at the well. Christ deliberately went through Samaria to meet with her—a route not often taken by the Jews because of the racial hatred between the two peoples. Yet He went because He had an appointment—an appointment to change one life to the glory of God the Father.

When Christ approached this woman she was in the process of drawing water to take to her home. Therefore He struck up a conversation on the simple subject at hand: water. He knew that she had gone to the depths of degradation in order to find a quenching for her thirst, but nothing she tried ever brought her lasting satisfaction. He suggested that she try some "living water," then promised her she would never thirst again.

His approach was so unsettling, yet so personal, that she found herself strangely drawn to this Christ. She did drink of the "water" He offered her, and she did find a quenching for her thirst. By any standard at all this was a successful witness.

Yet the Lord did not repeat this approach when He witnessed to Nicodemus. Instead of offering him "living

water" He told Nicodemus he had to be "born again."
Now Nicodemus was the only one in recorded Scripture
who received this particular injunction from Jesus. Why
did the Lord choose to use it with him and not with the
woman at the well? The answer is that Nicodemus was
trusting in his birthright as a Jew to grant him entrance into
eternal life. Therefore, Jesus had to say to him, "No,
Nicodemus, your physical birth is not enough. You need
to have another birth" (see John 3:3). The woman at the
well, in contrast, had no birthright of which to boast. Her
situation was entirely different. Jesus ministered specifically to each need. Notice, however, that the message in both
cases is the same: We need to be rightly related to the
Saviour. Only the phraseology is different. Yet that difference is the key to the heart.

Unfortunately, modern-day Christians have picked up
the phrase "born-again" from the story of Nicodemus and
for some reason think they haven't witnessed if they have-
n't used it somewhere along the line. Nonsense. There are
as many phrases to describe the Christian experience as
there are people to whom to describe it. For example,
salvation is freedom from the prison of self. It is direction
through the maze of life. It is peace in the eye of the storm.
It is healing for cancer of the soul. It is light in the midst of
darkness. It is a filling of the vacuum in a soul. It is having
one's life in tune. It is all these things and more. The
challenge lies in selecting the right analogy to meet the
need of the moment. Christ did and His ministry was
effective.

Christ was especially sensitive when He came to the
end of His conversations. Sometimes He deliberately let
the sinner go home with the question of his salvation
unresolved. Some people need a chance to think things
over a bit. Christ recognized this need. He also rested in
the fact that the Father is controlling the whole witnessing

process. He said, with a sense of perfect peace, "All that the Father gives Me will come to Me" (John 6:37). Thus He was under no salesman's pressure to force the sinner to "close the deal."

Christ's witness with the woman at the well is a good example of the absence of any invitation. The conversation ends with Christ's declaration that He is the Messiah. To those words there is no recorded response. As a matter of fact the only way we know that the woman did respond positively is through her actions. She began introducing other people to her Messiah.

The account of Christ's witness to Nicodemus leaves us hanging also. We know what Christ said to him, but we don't know how Nicodemus responded. The Lord did not manipulate him into making a decision right there on the spot. In fact, as far as we know, it took Nicodemus a couple of years to declare his new faith publicly. It is not until we watch him remove Christ's body from the cross that we learn of his commitment to serve his Lord at any cost.

These examples do not mean that we should always refrain from "closing the deal." On the contrary, some people need help. They simply do not know how to go about becoming a new creature in Christ. What these examples do teach us, though, is that we need to be sensitive to the inquirer's feelings as he is approached by the Lord who died for him.

If we are truly relying on the Holy Spirit not only to prepare men's hearts to receive the gospel but also to give us the right words to present it, then we are as free as Jesus Christ was to be creative in our approach to different individuals. There are certain basic truths, however, that we all need to have at our fingertips when our witness has progressed to the point of decision. We do not want to flounder at this critical time. So I am going to point out these truths and then give you a Scripture verse to support each one I mention. Then you can jot them down in your Bible where they will be ready when you need them.

The first truth is the foundational premise of this book: man's chief end and purpose for living. Point out 1 Corinthians 10:31: *"Whatever you do, do all to the glory of God."* Starting with God's glory instead of with man's sin gives not only the right thrust to your witness but a positive emphasis as well.

Somewhere in the discussion with your inquirer, however, he must see that his sin is keeping him from fulfilling this God-given goal. At this point you will need the following verses: *"For all have sinned and fall short of the glory of God"* (Rom. 3:23). Then show that there is a penalty for sin: *"For the wages of sin is death"* (Rom. 6:23).

These preliminaries bring you to the heart of the gospel: the ministry of Jesus Christ. Explain that Christ died on the cross to pay the penalty for man's sin: *"But God demonstrates His own love toward us in that while we were still sinners, Christ died for us"* (Rom. 5:8). Explain further that Christ's death on the cross has no personal efficacy until the individual receives the gift of eternal life, which is the Lord of glory Himself: *"But as many as received Him, to them He gave the right to become children of God, even to those who believe in His name"* (John 1:12).

At this point be flexible. For most people the act of conversion is a very sacred thing. Interference may be resented. If, however, the inquirer asks for help it is perfectly all right to give it. Some people have never prayed before, especially out loud. In this case suggest a spontaneous expression of commitment to God. "God, be merciful to me a sinner and save me for Jesus' sake" says everything that needs to be included. No matter how simple the words are, if repentance is evident, God is already working the miracle of regeneration. Just make sure it is God, not you, who is precipitating the new birth. You are not the life-giver. You are only the midwife.

Now your greatest challenge comes. *Resist the temptation to confirm salvation.* You must recognize the fact that the act of praying a prayer is not to be equated with new birth. Indeed there are people who pray the sinner's prayer and salvation is wrought within their souls. But there are other people who pray the same prayer and no change at all takes place. I remember the false profession of my own walk down the aisle. It is not the profession of the mouth but the condition of the heart that makes the difference. Jesus was more aware of this fact than anybody. He referred time and time again to people who were professing His Lordship with their mouths but, inside, their hearts were far from pure. Since you do not possess the ability to read anybody else's heart it is best to stay out of the business of confirming anyone's salvation. I am convinced that the success of John Palmer's witness with me is the fact that although I was professing to be a Christian he kept working with me as if I might be a heathen.

You do, however, want any genuine convert to know that it is possible to have assurance of eternal life. The Bible says, *"These things I have written to you who believe in the name of the Son of God, that you may KNOW that you have eternal life"* (1 John 5:13, emphasis mine). But you also want him to know that it is the Holy Spirit's job, not yours, to give that assurance: *"The Spirit Himself bears witness with our spirit that we are children of God"* (Rom. 8:16).

Make sure you lead your convert into the Word of God. There the Spirit's confirmation will come quite naturally. Explain to the new believer that he needs the food of the Scriptures just as much as he needs the food of the supermarket. Stress the importance of learning to pray to the Lord who holds his future. Encourage attendance at a Bible-preaching church and, if possible, membership in a small-group Bible study as well. Tell the young Christian that new birth means a brand new life. Hating the things he used to love and loving the things he used to hate will be the greatest confirmation that he is now a child of God. Jesus Christ stressed all these truths. That's why His true followers grew strong in their faith.

The Lord was an exemplary witness. His entire life was committed to bringing glory to His Father. Concerned less about the number of conversions He effected than about the quality of ministry He conducted, Christ selectively limited His involvement with people. Those with whom He did become involved received a warm, personal approach, tailored to their individual needs. In this approach the Galilean was so effective that certain people found themselves virtually drawn into His kingdom by an unseen magnet of love. In every aspect of His outreach Christ rested in the sovereignty of God, letting His Father's glory shine through His own natural way with people. What a perfect example to follow! What an exciting life to imitate!

Study Questions

1. Which type of ministry do you feel is more effective: a selective one that sometimes turns people away or a non-selective one that never says no to a need? Why?

2. How did Christ turn the subject of His conversations with non-believers to spiritual matters? Give some examples.

3. What concepts must be grasped before a person can receive Jesus Christ as his Saviour and Lord?

NINETEEN

Reaching My Neighborhood

The Bible commands, "Declare his glory among the heathen, his wonders among all people" (Ps. 96:3). These are rather awesome words to most Christians, especially those who have not been steeped in missionary emphasis. To me, when I was a brand new believer in Christ, they seemed so impossible to fulfill that I found them easy to dismiss. After all, I reasoned, God has seasoned Christians in His vineyard. Let some of *them* go and "declare his glory among the heathen."

Then one day the Lord became quite personal in His command. On a Tuesday morning while I was quietly ironing in my basement, a wild idea suddenly passed through my mind. Now I realize that the source of ideas is difficult to pinpoint. But I knew immediately that this one did not originate with me. You see, implementing the idea would require me to sacrifice my time, my interests, and my reputation. Believe me, I don't think up projects that cause me that much trouble. So I concluded that the idea came from the Lord.

Actually the "idea" took the form of a conversation: "Peg," the Lord said, addressing me directly, "you've been having coffee with your new neighbors for several months now, but you've never talked to them about me. Why don't you start a neighborhood Bible coffee and use it for my glory? You may find that teaching the Bible is your spiritual gift."

I was quick with my rebuttal. "Lord, I couldn't possibly do that. I have a husband and baby who need my attention. And I'm a very quiet person. I could never go to a neighbor's house and invite her to a Bible study. Besides, what if she came? The only part of the Bible I know anything at all about is the Gospel of John; and the only reason I know that is because John Palmer has been teaching it to me. I could never answer my neighbors' questions. What do you want me to do? Make a fool of myself on my very own street? No, I won't start a Bible study, Lord. Please don't ask me again."

Well, the Lord didn't ask me again. Not for a week anyway. Then the next Tuesday when I was ironing, the same "small voice" began to speak. This time it wasn't, "Why don't you start a neighborhood Bible coffee?" It was, "You really *ought* to start a neighborhood Bible coffee."

I protested. "Lord, I will not do that! The cost is too high. My neighbors will think I'm nuts. Besides, I don't even like coffee."

In God's mercy He let me live. For another week at least. Then He spoke again. This time it wasn't, "Why don't you. . . ?" or "You really ought to . . ." It was *"Thou shalt* start a neighborhood Bible coffee."

What do you do when God speaks to you like that? Over the previous three weeks this thought of a Bible study had mushroomed so greatly in my mind that I could hardly think of anything else. At night I even dreamed of Bible studies—all kinds of Bible studies. When the "voice" came again, this time in the form of a command, it scared me to death. I had heard of second chances. But how many people get *three* opportunities to obey the mandate of the Lord?

I was caught in a terrible bind. I felt if I didn't obey I might end up like Jonah—in the belly of a great "prepared

fish." And with my claustrophobia that was no place to be!
But if I did obey I'd be labeled a fanatic by the people I
wanted to reach the most. What was I supposed to do?

I knew that the Bible was my only rule for faith and
practice so I flew to the Scriptures with my dilemma.
Frantically I searched for a verse that would release me
from my obvious responsibility. I couldn't find one. Who
ever heard of the Lord saying, "Thou shalt *not* start a
neighborhood Bible study?"

In my dismay I found instead, "Arise and go . . . ye
shall be witnesses first in Jerusalem, then in Judea, then in
Samaria" (see Acts 1:8). I cried, "First in Jerusalem? First
on my very own street?"

In desperation I threw myself at the feet of Jesus.
"Lord, help me," I pleaded and really meant it. "I want to
obey your command with everything that is in me, but you
are asking me to do something that I am simply powerless
to do."

God said, "Good. I've been waiting for you to say that.
If you could do the task that I'm calling you to do your
ability would get in my way. Remember it's not your
strength that I want. It's your weakness. For in your weakness my strength is made perfect" (see 2 Cor. 12:9).

This time I couldn't say anything. I meekly accepted
God's promise of strength. But I must admit I surely didn't
notice the effect of that strength, not right away at least. It
was sheer obedience that pushed me out the door and
nudged me step by step across the street. I was shaking all
over, so much so in fact that I hoped my voice wouldn't
betray my fears. I guess it didn't. Because when I broached
the subject of a Bible study with Jerry, my neighbor, she
responded warmly. She told me she had been dabbling in
all sorts of cults and was willing to look for truth anywhere.
She said she'd come. I gasped, "You will?" Several other
neighbors responded positively too.

The first day our group met, everything seemed to go wrong. The first mistake was that the study was being held at my house; and I, as well as being the teacher, was also responsible for being the hostess. That meant that every time the phone or the doorbell rang I had to interrupt the study to answer it. I was up and down constantly.

The second problem was harder to handle. The cultists got off on tangents. The strong denominationalists started pushing their pet doctrines. And I found myself preaching at, instead of sharing with, my captive audience. In spite of all this, my own special miracle occurred: Jerry gave her heart to the Lord. It was a special seal on a ministry that God would continue to bless.

That first neighborhood Bible study did not explode into a burst of glory overnight. Along with the interruptions and doctrinal biases there was the problem of what to do with our children. Most of us were young mothers on very tight financial budgets. We simply couldn't afford baby-sitters every week. So we took our children with us almost everywhere we went. Since the Bible study was always at my house, my one-year-old was host to the gang. No mother really wanted to miss the study to baby-sit, so the toddlers were pretty much on their own. We put them in a spare room, threw in lots of toys, and quickly shut the door on the chaos. Then we prayed that they wouldn't kill each other. Most of the time we conducted our study in relative peace. If any of the children screamed the mother who recognized the voice would run into the room to establish order. I do not recommend this method of caring for the children of mothers attending a Bible study. But we were young and dumb and God was very good. We had no emergencies that I can remember.

Anyway, the children started looking forward to their weekly unsupervised play, the mothers were genuinely enjoying getting out of their houses on a regular basis, and

I was learning a lot about how *not* to lead a neighborhood Bible study. We met regularly for three or four years. Then, just as I was becoming an expert on the "don'ts" of leadership we moved to a brand new neighborhood and I had to start all over again.

I didn't really *want* to start all over again. But that biblical injunction was still very present within me: "Declare his glory among the heathen, his wonders among all people." Since I was as hesitant as usual about contacting neighbors for the Lord I recruited some help for myself. I found out who the other Christians were in my neighborhood, chose one of them and asked her if she would be willing to be the hostess for a neighborhood Bible study. She was delighted and quite excited about the adventure. Besides, she had a mother who just loved to baby-sit with children. "Thank you, Lord," I found myself whispering.

This time there were two of us making contacts. Since Adele, the hostess, was much better at the technique of inviting than I was, she got a greater response. That first meeting was quite a gathering. There were two Roman Catholics, two Greek Orthodox, two members of the Church of Christ, one Seventh Day Adventist, one Baptist, one Episcopalian, one Pentecostal, one die-hard legalist, one liberal Protestant, one Hebrew Christian (the hostess), and me. By the time all had made their introductions I didn't know what to call myself. I became an interdenominationalist right then and there and have tried to remain one ever since.

Every meeting was a challenge for me. Although I was beginning to feel that teaching might be my spiritual gift, I wanted to learn how to speak "the truth in love" (Eph. 4:15). And I actually got better at it as time went on. Oh, every once in a while I would lose my cool and get defensive. Then God would set me down and say, "Peg, my Word stands alone quite nicely. It needs no defense from anyone, especially you. Please remember that as you teach."

Believe me, I have remembered it. Now I no longer defend the Word of God. I simply present it. If anybody wants to fight, I let him fight with the Lord.

This second neighborhood group grew faster than the first had grown. In fact, it got too big to fit into Adele's home anymore. So we split into two groups and a new Christian who was growing nicely in the Lord took the responsibility of teaching the second group.

Then another exciting thing happened. The men, who were seeing changes wrought in their wives, decided that they would like a group of their own. So my husband, who loves to share Christ with businessmen anyway, gathered them together around the Word of God. Now he too was faced with a challenge: two Roman Catholics, one Greek Orthodox, one interested Hebrew . . .

The groups met faithfully for years. The men were so addicted to their fellowship that they would often cut business trips short just to make their Monday night meeting. Then it became necessary for our family to move again. The leaving this time was harder. The distance was greater and the ties were stronger. But we left knowing that lives had been changed by the Saviour, and many were growing in His likeness.

After we got established in our new neighborhood, halfway across the country from the old one, we knew God would have us put our experience to use. Author Gladys Hunt advises: "When you move into a new neighborhood, look for the people whom God is drawing to Himself." I find this a very exciting project. The only trouble is after doing it for several years now I've learned that the ones who at first appearance look to me as if they're being drawn are not really being drawn at all. In fact, I find that God is usually working in the life of someone I have crossed off my list of possibilities. This witnessing business is humbling.

My third neighborhood Bible study had as many problems getting started as the first two, only this time the problems were of a different sort. Again I teamed up with a hostess. And again we invited our neighbors. I had still not become good at issuing invitations but together Judy and I let it be known that we were holding a Bible study, and the Lord drew several neighbors to Judy's house. By the time I faced this third group of neighbors I had learned how to skirt doctrinal issues—well, *almost* learned. And all our children were now either in school or married so we didn't have the problem of rounding up baby-sitters anymore.

Our frustration was one of numbers. There were weeks when the group was so small that it was embarrassing to teach a lesson. I mean, how do you face only two other bodies and present your material in such a way that those bodies don't feel threatened? I kept reminding the Lord that this was my third study and we should be doing much better than we were, but He didn't seem to appreciate my frustrations. There were days when I wanted to quit altogether. If it hadn't been for Judy I would have. Her commitment kept me faithful to finish what we had begun.

The second year our group grew bigger. The third year we grew bigger still. By the time we were ending our fifth year of study we had grown too large for Judy's living room. Also by this time I was being asked to speak at so many other functions that something had to go from my schedule. After much prayer Judy and I decided to discontinue the neighborhood Bible study. We felt that there is a time to start and a time to stop. This seemed to be the time to stop. We knew that the seed had been sown and the harvest would come whether we were present to witness it or not. And we comforted ourselves in the fact that many precious memories would accompany us into eternity.

Over the years God has confirmed to both of us the fact that we made the right decision, for the two of us are presently pursuing equally exciting but totally different ministries.

I have included this personal experience not to suggest that God wants to use you in the same way He is using me, but to illustrate that God can use anyone, even reluctant vessels, to reach into the world with His glory. That means He can use you too. Don't be like me though: stubborn, rebellious, and needing to be pushed. Yield your will to the will of your Lord. Just bow your head and say, "Lord Jesus, I'm yours. Use me in any way that is pleasing to you." Then listen intently for His instructions. Before long you will have discovered the marvelous truth that you too can "declare his glory among the heathen, his wonders among all people."

Study Questions

1. Name some of the different methods people use to reach their neighbors with the gospel. Which of these methods would you be most comfortable implementing?

2. Make a pro/con list for starting a Bible study in your neighborhood. Example: Pro: Neighbors might be saved; Con: Neighbors might think I'm a fanatic.

3. Why do you think Jesus told His disciples to witness first in Jerusalem before they witnessed in wider circles?

TWENTY

Venturing from the Nest

Venturing forth to share God's glory with others is very much like flying. It is absolutely terrifying at first but the more you do of it, the more you want to do. Of course, getting most Christians to the point of being able to fly at all takes quite a bit of encouragement. In fact, some of us need a shove from the nest.

In God's wonderful world of nature the bird family offers a good example of the trials and tribulations of flight training. Now everyone knows that birds are supposed to fly. But evidently the word hasn't reached every member of the bird world.

Anyway, the mother bird usually begins making preparations to receive trainees in her flight school long before applications for admission are even filed. Day after day she gathers sticks, leaves, and insulation—anything she can find to act as a buffer from the weather. Then when the last opening is filled, she stands back to admire her work. "Nice little dormitory," she boasts.

One day she lays her eggs. Shifting her weight from side to side she blankets every shell with the warmth of her downy feathers. Then she settles down contentedly to wait for the process of reproduction to take its natural course.

As the days pass slowly by she patiently remains on the nest. All of a sudden new life begins to stir in one of the shells. There's a trial tap on the enclosure. Then a determined pecking. A hairline crack appears. Then an actual opening. Bit by bit a form emerges—scrawny, naked, and trembling. As it struggles to support its weight it seems bewildered by the expanse of the new world it has entered. It is helpless and alone, yet quite happy to be alive. The mother, sensing her youngster's fear, snuggles it gently under her wing. Quietly it settles there. Soon other birds emerge to join the contented family.

From the vantage point of the ground the nest seems to be filled with mouths. They are always open, squawking constantly for food. Dutifully the mother flies away and dutifully she returns to stuff the little caverns. Then she flies away again and stuffs the mouths some more. Even though it seems like a hopeless task the mother bird keeps right on stuffing.

It doesn't take the babies very long to realize that they've got a good thing going. They're protected, they're warm, they're full, and they're pampered. Why, it would be fun to stay in the nest forever!

One day the mother bird senses a crisis. Her babies are getting too fat. In fact, they've actually grown bigger than she is. For the observer it borders on hilarity to watch a sleek mother bird jamming food into the beak of a fledgling that is half again her size. For the mother bird, however, it is a moment of concern. She suddenly realizes that if the present trend continues, her babies will never be able to raise their weighty bodies into the air. So she immediately gives them a lesson in how to flex their wings.

Then one day she announces, "This is it, kids. Line up. You're about to learn how to fly."

Most of the fledglings are ready to go. They've been waiting a long time for this day. There are a couple of kids in every family, however, who are scared to death to take chances.

"Not me," cries one young bird. "Not today. I'm not

ready to fly today. I haven't had any lessons. I might run into a storm. I don't know how to land. And besides, I'd rather stay in the nest."

Now if the mother bird were of the permissive school of child rearing she would listen to her youngster and say, "OK, Fraidy, you don't have to fly today. You can fly whenever you feel like it." And the baby would probably continue to stay in its nest all the rest of its life. Even if it did decide to fly later, by then it would no doubt be too bulky to lift its weight off the branch.

Fortunately, the mother bird is not permissive in the raising of her young. She nudges the frightened youngster to the edge of the branch and then, amid much squawking, gently pushes him off. At this point the "impossible" occurs. The reluctant bird spreads its wings and actually flies. Why does it fly? Because it has to. You see, it either flies or it dies.

This is how I view my own relationship to God. He takes care of me just as diligently as the mother bird takes care of her frightened fledgling. Long before the foundation of the world my Father made plans for my spiritual birth. Carefully He built the situation that would someday effect my salvation. Then one day He planted in me the seed of His living Word, and when the time was right He watched me peck my way out of self into the freedom of everlasting life.

At first I had my mouth open constantly. I was hungry for the Word all the time. Diligently my heavenly Father fed me with nuggets of truth from the Scriptures. It didn't take me long to realize that I had a good thing going with my Lord. I was protected. I was full. And I was happy. And I was in danger of staying in my cozy little nest for the rest of my spiritual life.

Then one day the Lord said, "Fly!" When I heard the command I felt just as stubborn as the baby bird that talked back to its mother. "I'm not ready to fly," I argued. "I've never had a flying lesson in my life. Besides, I don't have time to fly. I have a husband and a child and hobbies. I also have a reputation to protect. What if I tried to fly and failed? People would laugh at me. You'll never get me off this branch. I simply am not going to fly!"

I'm glad God was not too permissive with me. As you know He did let me rebel for a while. One day, though, He gently pushed me from the nest. And He's been urging me on ever since.

When I got shoved out, I flew. Not because I wanted to but because I had to. For me, as for the bird, it was fly or die. By "die" I don't mean to imply that if I had disobeyed God's command I would have been in danger of losing His grace in my life. No. My salvation rests securely in heaven. But I do mean that I would have lost the opportunity of glorifying God as He wished to be glorified through me at that particular time. My testimony would have shriveled. My chance for future outreach might have died.

You know, it's really fun to fly. There's no other way to learn how to do it than to spread your spiritual wings and leap out of the security of your nest. Then you learn that the air is really your element. You were made for the purpose of flying.

I don't mean to suggest that there are no problems in learning to fly. On the contrary; there are headwinds that shift you off course and storms that would force you from the sky. There is heat that saps the moisture from your body and distances far greater than you feel you can cover alone. But just when you think about returning to the nest and never venturing forth from your backyard again you pick up the tailwind of the Holy Spirit of God and you soar to the regions beyond.

After a while you get quite proficient at the exciting art of flying. You learn how to turn and dip and dive and climb. You learn how high you can go without fainting and how long you can glide without flapping. You learn how to use the air currents to your advantage and the weather patterns for your safety. And all of this takes place in God's sky.

I'm glad God saw the danger of my staying too long in the nest. I truly love to feed on the living Word of God. If the Lord hadn't intervened and shown me how to work off some of my rich Bible learning through exercise I would still be home in my easy chair having my private devotions with the Lord. And I'd be getting fatter and fatter by the hour. By now I probably would have accumulated a tremendous amount of deep truth. I would have escaped the embarrassment of sharing the gospel with neighbors and the burden of praying that God would meet their needs. I would have avoided a few discussions that proved fruitless and a host of sleepless hours wondering who would show up for the study the next day. I would have had much more time for my hobbies and a chance to go to lunch with my friends.

But I also would have missed one of the most exciting opportunities ever offered me to glorify God with my life. I would have missed seeing what the power of the Word can do through someone as weak as I. I would have missed seeing a marriage restored through a study we did on forgiveness. I would have missed hearing a mother tell how her prodigal daughter had returned home because our group had fervently prayed. I would have missed watching searching eyes light up as truth suddenly all fit together. In short, I would have missed the marvelous adventure of flying in God's vast, limitless sky.

Reader, be sure you don't miss whatever God has for you. One of these days He is going to say, "Fly." For some of you that command may mean, "Leave the security of your religiosity and trust me alone with your life." For others of you it may be an injunction to get down on your knees in prayer or into the Word of God on a daily, regular basis. For still others it may mean joining an organization and giving your all for the glory of God.

Whatever God says when He speaks directly to you, of one thing I am certain: Your status quo will be shaken! Your normal routine will be shattered! Your values will be turned end over end! Furthermore, this upheaval will be the best thing that has ever happened to you.

As you lift your wings to glorify God in the way He specifies for you, you will experience the joy of knowing that you are fulfilling the purpose for which you were created. But your exuberance will not stop there. You will have the thrill of seeing God do through you what you could never do by yourself. Listen to yourself saying, "Hey, look, I can fly!" It is an experience without equal on this earth.

Dangers will come, to be sure; but now you know the One who can bring you safely through them. He hears your every cry: "These winds—they're shifting me off course. Save me, Lord! Get me back on the beam." In a flash He'll be right by your side, loving you, energizing you, and preparing you for the task of showing others how to fly. Oh, they won't all be interested in learning. But that is really not your concern. It is God's.

As for you, you will just keep on flying. You will keep on because you know that you must. You will fly through darkness as well as through sunshine, through storms as well as through calm, when you are tired as well as when you are refreshed, when you are old as well as when you are young. Nothing will be able to thrust you from the sky because God Himself made you for flying. You will fly and fly and fly until you think you can fly no more. Then just when you are about to give up in exhaustion you will hear a still, small voice of promise: "They that wait upon the

Lord shall renew their strength; they shall mount up with wings as eagles; they shall run, and not be weary; and they shall walk, and not faint" (Isa. 40:31).

Then when the voice has ceased its speaking you will receive the thrill of your life. You will find that where you have flown is right into the arms of your Lord. "And the glory of the Lord shall be revealed, and all flesh shall see it together: for the mouth of the Lord hath spoken it" (Isa. 40:5). Amen.

Study Questions

1. What are some of the nests of security in your life?

2. Name the hazards of remaining too long in these nests. Of venturing out of these nests.

3. What are the rewards in both cases? Which rewards are greatest? Why?

Conclusion

Dear reader, I must end with a word of caution. Although the last chapter of this book is obviously an "action" chapter, I do not mean to imply that to glorify God with your life you have to be "doing" something all the time. On the contrary, I feel that God is much more interested in what we are *becoming* than in what we are *doing* for His sake. Glorifying God is essentially reflecting His righteousness and holiness. It is possible to do that just as effectively in a quiet way as it is to do it in an aggressive way.

Certainly we all want to be used of God. We have learned that sharing our faith is one way He uses us. But remember we share through living as well as through going somewhere and preaching. You may be reading this book from a bed of affliction. For you "flying" may simply be persevering through your pain, refusing to stop trusting the One who promises to meet your every need. Or you may be reeling from the "untimely" death of a loved one. At the moment you are going through a patch of darkness. Don't forget that those who keep on "flying" eventually reach the light beyond. Or you may be in a state of consternation, wondering how God can possibly use the mess you are in to bring glory to His name.

Well, He can. In fact, that is the real message of this book. God has given us a purpose for our lives that we cannot accomplish in our own strength. We cannot even accomplish it with God's help. Only *He* can accomplish it. And that miracle occurs when we totally abandon ourselves to *His* purposes and let Him accomplish it *through* us.

To this end I offer a prayer from my heart: O God, I want to behold you in all your awesome majesty. I want to behold you that way every day. Keep me faithful in reading your Word, Lord, so faithful, in fact, that by beholding your image in the Scriptures I myself become a reflection of that image. As I read, grant that I will become so filled with the Scriptures that your words rise back up to you as prayers. Father, I want to become your channel—your channel of blessing to others.

Give me an appreciation of myself as you see me: a vessel weak in itself but empowered by your strength; a flower that is fading more and more each day but carries the potential for new life tucked within its soul; a garment that is lifeless until Life itself invades it; a part of your Body, the church, with a spiritual gift all my own; a sinner exalted to the position of saint. O Lord, how much I have in you!

Help me to guard everything that I have been given. Make me aware of the dangers that would rob me. Don't let the pressure cooker of life crush my faith. Rescue me from the trivialities of the moment, reminding me that in every situation eternity's values are at stake. Keep my eyes so fixed on you that I am not distracted by the temptations of this world. And give me the discernment that I need to tell the difference between those who would strengthen my faith and those who would lead me astray.

Give me your grace in my outreach to others. As you know there will be times when you will have to nudge me to get going. Please make me sensitive to those nudges and willing to respond. When I do respond, help that response to be natural, flowing freely through the personality that you have given me. So that I don't get overextended in my ministry, teach me where my priorities lie and how to control my opportunities for maximum effectiveness. And may I make an ongoing effort to keep my testimony beyond reproach. For I want to reflect without distortion the radiance of your glory.

Don't ever let me forget what I'm supposed to be doing here on this earth, leaving me with the shame of "Ichabod" written over my life. I remember how you wrote that word over Israel's defeat at the hand of the Philistine army, "the glory has departed" (see 1 Sam. 4:21,22). How sad! In Israel's case I surmise that the cause of your displeasure was not so much the defeat itself as the fact that the ark of the covenant had been taken by the enemy—the ark where your Word was housed. Don't let your Word be stolen like that from my life, Lord, by the selfish demands of people or by lack of time or by too many obligations or by an overextended outreach. Keep me faithful to guard my quiet hour with you, for I realize how important personal devotions really are to a life that wants to glorify God.

I'm right back at the point where I started this book—right back to the importance of your life-changing Word. Keep me in it always, I beg you, O Lord—studying it, assimilating it, trusting it, and praying it. Use it to uplift me during my periods of depression. For there are times when I feel like giving up. Use it to remind me, as you are reminding me even now, that I will eventually be what you want me to be—not because of *my* work for you but because of *your* work in me. How I praise you for such a powerful book! For through it I am actually being changed—from glory to glory to glory to glory—"even as by the Spirit of the Lord." And I know that this is only the beginning. For one day the last trump shall sound and I shall be changed one more time—permanently—as you call me unto your *eternal* glory.

Meanwhile, I commit myself afresh to you—"to you who are able to keep me from falling, to you who have promised to present me faultless before the presence of your glory with exceeding joy, to you the only wise God my Saviour.

"To you be glory and majesty and dominion and power both now and ever. Amen" (see Jude 24,25).